A Guide to
SCENES &
MONOLOGUES
from Shakespeare
and His Contemporaries

Kurt Daw • Julia Matthews

HEINEMANN • Portsmouth, NH

HEINEMANN
A division of Reed Elsevier Inc.
361 Hanover Street
Portsmouth, NH 03801–3912

Offices and agents throughout the world

Library of Congress Cataloging-in-Publication Data
Daw, Kurt.
    A guide to scenes and monologues from Shakespeare and his contemporaries / Kurt Daw, Julia Matthews
        p.   cm.
    Includes bibliographic references.
    ISBN 0-325-00015-8
    1. Acting—Auditions.   2. Shakespeare, William 1564–1616—Outlines, syllabi, etc.
    I. Matthews, Julia.   II. Title.
    PN2080.D38   1998
    792.9'5' 09421—dc21   97-52066
                                                                    CIP

Editor: Lisa A. Barnett
Production: Abigail M. Heim
Cover design: Julie Nelson Gould
Manufacturing: Louise Richardson

Printed in the United States of America on acid free paper

02   01   00   99   98   DA   1   2   3   4   5   6   7   8   9

For our students

Contents

Acknowledgments

This book grew out of many conversations and experiments with our friends and colleagues in the 1995–96 "Shakespeare Examined Through Performance" Institute, which took place at the Folger Institute under the auspices of the National Endowment for the Humanities. Alan Dessen and Audrey Stanley, the leaders of the workshop, inspired us to search for ways to bring intellectual devotion into theatrical production and theatrical creativity into scholarship and teaching. The participants in this workshop, most of whom read and commented on this work in its formative stages, include Cezarija Abartis, Eric Binnie, Sheila Cavanagh, Daniel Colvin, Tom Gandy, Miranda Johnson-Haddad, Edward Isser, Robert Lane, Caroline McManus, Paul Nelsen, Edward Rocklin, Ellen Summers, William Taylor, and Clare-Marie Wall, with sterling support from the Folger Institute staff of Lena Cowen Orlin, Kathleen Lynch, Carol Brobeck, and Rebecca Willson. In particular we thank Edward Isser and Paul Nelsen for their close reading and insightful comments in the development of this manuscript. We are grateful to the librarians at Kennesaw State University and Emory University for their kindness, to our colleague Connie Johnson for her patient and resourceful help in completing the work at Kennesaw, and to Lisa Barnett for her skillful editing at Heinemann. Finally we thank our students, who inspire us every day with their energy and insight.

Introduction

Some of the richest dramatic material in the English language comes from the plays of Shakespeare and his contemporaries. Any actor interested in the classical theater will relish the vibrant characters and their passionate, opulent language. This volume guides actors through the drama of Shakespeare's day. The chapters introduce the predominant styles and genres of the English and Spanish stages, as well as the major playwrights and their plays. Each chapter also provides a detailed list of scenes and monologues from this exciting repertoire, which are also categorized in convenient indexes. Whether you are looking for audition material, scenes for acting class, or simply a broader understanding of the drama of Shakespeare's time, this book will point you toward fresh, provocative, and meaty selections.

This book is organized according to the dramatic genres of comedy, tragedy, history, and romance customarily associated with the plays of Shakespeare. Each section begins with a brief description of what these categories meant in the early modern (Elizabethan and Jacobean) periods, which is often slightly different from what they mean to audiences today. By comparing plays of a similar genre, patterns of theatrical development emerge, and thinking about these patterns can be very productive for actors. By considering plays and scenes this way, actors should be able to make some basic decisions about approaches and style.

Each chapter presents a group of Shakespeare's plays, followed by comparable plays by his contemporaries, accompanied by biographical introductions to each new playwright. Therefore, actors can look beyond familiar selections into additional possibilities from plays they may not know, listed on the nearby pages. From each play actors will find a list of excerpts suitable for auditions, monologue work, and scene study. The notation for these scene and monologue selections is discussed below.

This book is a companion volume to *Acting Shakespeare and His Contemporaries*, by Kurt Daw, which leads actors through a series of exercises. In keeping with the material discussed there, this companion volume provides references to sonnets, monologues, intimate scenes (in which only two or three characters are present), and public scenes (in which the conversation between two characters takes place in public, before bystanders).

Finally, this volume includes a brief introduction to the drama of the Spanish Golden Age. Roughly contemporaneous with Shakespeare's age, the Spanish drama shares the exciting action, opulent language, and fluid staging conventions of its English counterpart. In Chapter 5, we suggest a few possibilities for exploring this rich repertoire in English translations.

How the Notation Works

Under the headings of a dramatist and a particular play title you will find information about specific monologues and scenes. Monologues are listed by their act number in large Roman numerals, their scene number in small roman numerals, and, for Shakespeare monologues only, the line numbers from the scene in Arabic numerals. The character name is given, followed by the first line of the speech, and a brief description of its content. Here's an example of a monologue selection from Shakespeare's *As You Like It*, listed in the Comedy chapter:

III.ii.359–382 Rosalind: "Love is merely a madness"*
In disguise, Rosalind speaks her mind on the vagaries of love.

For all Shakespearean selections, the act, scene and line numbers are keyed to the 1997 *Norton Shakespeare*. Therefore, in that edition, you will find this speech in Act III, Scene ii, from lines 359–382. Please note that these numbers may differ slightly from those found in other editions. This should not overly concern you. Even with another edition, you can usually find the speech or scene quickly by looking for the act/scene/line referenced and then scanning over the nearby material.

Plays by Shakespeare's contemporaries cannot be keyed to some standard line index, and for that reason, monologues are simply referenced by act and scene number, plus first lines.

For scene suggestions, you will see an act and scene number, followed by a short description that indicates the characters and the situation. Here's a non-Shakespearean example from Beaumont and Fletcher's tragicomedy, *Philaster*:

II.ii. *The lustful Spanish prince Pharamond seduces Megra, a lady attending his betrothed.*

Speech and scene references that are followed by an asterisk (*) require some minor editing (perhaps to delete an interruption).

Those that begin with struck-through characters should start with the words immediately following the strike-throughs. The purpose of this notation is to suggest a mid-line start to a piece that begins with extraneous material.

After finding a scene or monologue suggestion that looks interesting, you will need to find a copy of the play. We recommend the new 1997 *Norton Shakespeare*. This edition is based on entirely new editing of Shakespeare's plays using the Folio as a control text. It is far more actor-friendly than many older editions, which are more commonly written for the benefit of scholars. If you can't find, or don't want, the Norton, you may well want to look into the second edition of the *Riverside Shakespeare*. This work carries a fine reputation. Whatever edition you choose, look for evidence that the scholarship is current and the editorial principles are clearly stated. Beware of inexpensive editions, as they are often inaccurate and misleading. For finding the plays of Shakespeare's contemporaries, please consult the following notes.

Notes on Editions of the Plays of Shakespeare's Contemporaries

You can probably find an inexpensive modern edition of any of Shakespeare's plays at your local bookstore. However, it may take more effort to find the plays of Shakespeare's contemporaries. Don't be discouraged; with a little perseverance you should be able to locate any of the plays listed in this book. The following sections describe the kinds of editions in which the plays of the English Renaissance appear.

Anthologies

General drama anthologies are likely to include only the best-known works of this period, such as Marlowe's *Doctor Faustus*, Jonson's *Volpone* or *The Alchemist*, Webster's *Duchess of Malfi*, or Kyd's *Spanish Tragedy*. More specialized anthologies of drama from the early modern period can be found in libraries and in academic bookstores. Some of the anthologies from the first half of the twentieth century contain remarkable collections, such as John S. Farmer's collections for the Early English Text Society, so don't be put off by the older volumes. While large anthologies are difficult to use in rehearsal because of their size and do not always provide the kind of detailed notes that actors might desire, they are nevertheless a useful way to track down potential material. A few smaller anthologies are available in paperback from academic publishers such as Penguin and Oxford, offering three or four plays according to genre (citizen comedies, revenge tragedies, and so forth).

Complete Works

Various scholars have laboriously collected the complete works of individual playwrights, usually in multivolume sets that you can find in libraries. (Most are too large and expensive to find in bookstores, although there are exceptions.) These collections are remarkable feats of scholarship and dedication, given the messy and often contradictory early editions and the difficulties of attributing authorship or composition date. Many Works preserve the period spelling and punctuation of their source editions for the sake of scholarly interest. This can be daunting to readers new to early modern studies, but these works may provide interesting indications of emphasis and rhythm.

Some of these collections are eighty to one hundred years old, and scholarly opinion about certain editorial decisions may have changed since the Works were published, but they are still prime sources for actors to search for material. If you can't find the play you are looking for within the Complete Works, you may need to look for it under another author's name. As with the Beaumont and Fletcher puzzle, authorship is not always easily identifiable.

Be aware that Complete Works means poetry and prose works as well as drama; if you have the option, choose the Complete Plays.

Selected Works

A more convenient option for surveying the major plays of a given playwright is to find a volume of his Selected Works. Several academic publishers such as Penguin, Everyman, and Oxford University Press, offer paperback books containing three or four plays by a particular dramatist, along with some supporting notes and introductory material. These are nice volumes to own because they are small enough to handle in rehearsal, yet offer a glimpse of the playwright's range and style. They are also more apt to use modern spelling and punctuation than are the scholarly editions. Libraries also carry larger hardback volumes of playwrights' selected works. Bear in mind that editors' selections are often based on literary rather than theatrical criteria, and that great scenes and monologues can often be pulled from "lesser" dramas.

Individual Plays

Individual scripts are by far the most convenient editions for actors. Ideally, actors would like editions that are light and small enough to carry in rehearsal, have helpful, practical notes, and have enough blank space to add their own notes. Fortunately, several publishers have created wonderful series of individual play scripts that have all this and more. The *Regents Renaissance Drama Series*, published by the University of Nebraska Press, and the *Revels Plays*, now managed by Manchester University Press/St. Martin's Press, brought out a number of careful editions of important English plays in modern spelling in the 1960s and 1970s. Manchester University Press has recently begun publishing the *Revels Student Editions*, a series of plays annotated for students rather than scholars. Yale University Press produced excellent individual editions in the Yale Ben Jonson series.

Some of these individual editions are still in print and can be ordered or purchased at academic and theatrical bookstores. Others can be found in academic libraries. However, even these fine series do not represent every early modern play, and some works can be found only in collections.

Facsimiles

As discussed in the *Acting Shakespeare and His Contemporaries* chapter on editions of Shakespeare, facsimiles of sixteenth- and seventeenth-century editions can be illuminating to the actor, especially when used in conjunction with a responsible modern edition. Facsimiles are available for some of the plays by Shakespeare's contemporaries. An extraordinary group of scholars, led by W. W. Greg, produced the series of individual facsimiles, known as the *Malone Society Reprints,* from the 1900s to 1930s. This groundbreaking series includes a number of anonymous plays. The Malone editions can be found in academic libraries. Many academic libraries are now able to provide facsimiles on microfilm and microfiche; while not very convenient for rehearsal use, these historical resources are well worth consulting as you prepare your role.

Monologue Collections

There are a number of volumes of monologues and scenes from early modern drama available on the market. Because they contain only a few selections, say twenty to thirty each, they are apt to lead you to seriously overperformed material. They also tend to be based on older editions of plays, so their editorial decisions are often very questionable. Their most serious drawback, however, is that they extract the speeches and scenes from the plays without offering much context. If you haven't read the play, how can you make intelligent decisions about your role? Use these books as a way to taste the distinctive flavors of the different dramatists, and then go find the plays themselves.

Comedies

*C*omedy is difficult to define in words. Theories of tragedy have abounded, starting with Aristotle's *Poetics*, but comedy is more difficult to pin down. Classical and medieval theories often described comedy in opposition to tragedy: the comic plot begins with a misfortune and ends with its successful resolution, not vice versa; comic characters are private citizens, not royalty, heroes, gods, or generals; comic language is humble and witty, not lofty. Surprisingly, *comedy* is not necessarily defined in terms of the laughter it provokes; for Shakespeare and his contemporaries, a play could be a comedy without being especially funny.

Fortunately, however, the dramatists of the sixteenth and seventeenth centuries did write many hilarious comedies. The comedies of the new professional theaters in London were cobbled together out of a wealth of comic sources: village folk plays, Christian mystery and miracle plays, allegorical morality plays, clowns' routines and jigs, Latin plays of Plautus and Terence (routinely taught to schoolboys), adaptations of classical comedies, newly published novels and stories, civic pageants, and elite entertainments at court. One of the most exciting aspects of studying Shakespeare's theater is to see the evolution of comic styles and forms as actors, audiences, and playwrights developed new plays to suit their tastes.

Early Comedies by Shakespeare (c. 1590–1595)

This first section looks at comedies written, scholars generally agree, early in Shakespeare's career. These plays deal with love and woo-ing, although some do so less overtly than others. In all of them, the comedic energy arises from misalignment rather than genuine con-flict. Characters in these plays usually want the same outcome, but because they express it differently, or come into important informa-tion at different times, or are simply misunderstood, they find them-selves at temporary odds with each other. There are no certified villains in these early comedies. These plays far more often portray characters in the process of self-discovery than characters overcom-ing obstacles and opposition.

Two Gentlemen of Verona (c. 1589)

Two Gentlemen of Verona is, by uncommon agreement, a young man's play. The plot concerns the relationship of the two young men of the title, Valentine and Proteus, and the conflict between friendship and love. It is, therefore, not just a play about very young men, but also one that, thematically, looks seriously at issues of adolescent adjust-ment into adulthood. Because of these aspects of the work, many suppose that this is Shakespeare's earliest extant play. It is certainly not unreasonable to speculate that this is a play by a young man, as well as about young men.

The romantic entanglements of the play are very complex. Each young man is in love, but the more changeable of the two (Proteus) determines to abandon his own love (Julia) in order to steal his friend's intended (Sylvia). Julia followers her love in disguise as a boy, a device that Shakespeare used often in his career. The unravel-ing of the love plot is the least satisfactory aspect of the play. Valen-tine not only forgives his friend for attempting to steal Sylvia, but also offers to give her up for his friend. Proteus makes a last-second decision to "do the right thing" and returns to Julia, who (like Sylvia) has stood by mutely throughout the final scene.

Although it lacks the plot control of Shakespeare's later plays, *Two Gentlemen of Verona* contains some beautiful poetry and some charming scenes. It also contains perhaps the one clown character, Lance (with his dog, Crab), that easily transcends time and, almost without assistance, remains funny today.

This play has wonderful material for young actors. The characters are witty and vivacious, and the play has an underpinning of serious emotional relationships. It also contains a large number of two-person scenes, which are good for scene study classes.

MONOLOGUE SUGGESTIONS

I.ii.99–100, 105–130. Julia: "This babble shall not henceforth trouble me."*
> *Julia attempts to read a letter she has torn into pieces in order to hide its importance from her maid.*

II.iv.185–207. Proteus: "Even as one heat another heat expels"
> *In soliloquy, Proteus reveals that he has fallen in love with Valentine's beloved.*

II.vi.1–43. Proteus: "To leave my Julia shall I be forsworn"
> *Proteus embarks on his campaign of betrayal.*

III.i.170–187. Valentine: "And why not death, rather than living torment?"
> *Banished, Valentine laments his fate.*

IV.iv.1–33. Lance: "When a man's servant shall play the cur with him"
> *Lance proves he has more loyalty for his dog than most characters in the play have for their loves.*

IV.iv.175–197. Julia: "Alas, how love can trifle with itself."
> *Julia compares herself to a portrait of her rival.*

INTIMATE SCENE SUGGESTIONS

I.i. *Valentine is parted from his best friend, Proteus, as he heads from Verona to Milan.*

I.i. *In the scene immediately following, Speed comically refuses to tell Proteus whether or not he delivered a love letter.*

I.ii. *The maid, Lucetta, teases her mistress, Julia, about a love letter she has intercepted.*

II.i. *Speed freely offers his opinions on Valentine's beloved.*

II.v. *Speed and Lance discuss their respective masters' romances.*

III.i. *The same two comedians consider a letter describing Lance's love.*
III.i. *The Duke tricks Valentine into revealing his plans to elope with the Duke's daughter Sylvia, for which he banishes him.*
IV.iv. *In her disguise as a page, Julia delivers a love letter from Proteus to Sylvia, though she loves him herself.*

The Comedy of Errors (c. 1592)

The other candidate for earliest comedy is *The Comedy of Errors*, a play clearly based on a classical model, Plautus' *Menaechmi Twins*, which Shakespeare may well have read in school in the original Latin. The plot concerns a set of identical twins, each named Antipholus, who were separated in a shipwreck at sea when children and have since been raised in distant (and enemy) cities. Improbably, but hilariously, their servants are also twins, each named Dromio, who were separated as children. When the twin and his servant raised in Syracuse land in Ephesus, they are constantly mistaken for their Ephesian counterparts. Likewise, the Ephesian master and servant are blamed for troubles started by their unknowing twins. Perhaps the greatest complications of the play involve the visiting Syracuse twin's romance with Luciana, his Ephesian brother's wife's sister. She, of course, is convinced she is being courted by her own brother-in-law and is torn by her conflicting feelings.

Despite its farcical framework, *The Comedy of Errors* convincingly tackles the issues of identity and belonging, and it has more depth and substance than you might expect. Pay special attention to the brilliant surprise ending. This is, by the way, the briefest of all Shakespeare plays, and though it contains few two-person scenes, there is plenty of good material for working on comic technique.

MONOLOGUE SUGGESTIONS

II.i.58–73. Dromio of Ephesus: "I mean not cuckold mad, but sure he is stark mad."*
   Dromio complains to his mistress of how he was beaten for calling his master to dinner.
II.ii.110–146. Adriana: "Ay, ay, Antipholus look strange and frown"
   A wife berates the man she thinks is her husband.

INTIMATE SCENE SUGGESTIONS
I.ii. *Antipholus of Syracuse mistakenly beats the thoroughly confused Dromio of Ephesus for losing (or perhaps stealing) his money.*
II.ii. *In the sequel to the previous scene, Antipholus of Syracuse quarrels with Dromio of Syracuse (his own servant), who has no idea what has happened with his twin.*
III.ii. *Luciana is shocked when Antipholus of Syracuse (whom she mistakenly thinks is her brother-in-law) tries to woo her.*
III.ii. *Dromio of Syracuse tells his master of his encounter with the enormous Nell.*

The Taming of the Shrew (c. 1592)

In Shakespeare's time, *The Taming of the Shrew* was probably a pleasant but slight work dealing with the simple story of a man who marries and tames a hot-tempered woman. In it, she comes to see the necessity of order and harmony and to appreciate the depths of her husband's character. "Shrew" plays are quite common throughout Europe during this period, and Shakespeare seems to have meant his play as one more example in a familiar genre.

In our time, when the relationship of the sexes is a hotly contested social issue, this play can present a lot of difficult issues. Productions frequently try to downplay the problems by concentrating on farce, or conversely, undercut the ending by suggesting that Kate is not truly tamed. The best recent productions, however, have faced the situation head-on and tried to discover how the intellectual match between equals is negotiated and confirmed.

The scene and monologue material from this play, particularly that involving the principals, can be extraordinarily rewarding to work on. Careful thought is required, however, about the intentions behind the actions. Ideology, as well as technique, is apt to become an important performance issue.

MONOLOGUE SUGGESTIONS
II.i.166–179. Petruccio: "I pray you do. I'll attend her here"
    Petruccio plans his strategy for his first meeting with Kate.
IV.i.169–192. Petruccio: "Thus have I politicly begun my reign"
    In a speech filled with images of falconry, Petruccio recounts his progress.

V.ii.140–182. Kate: "Fie, fie, unknit that threat'ning unkind brow"
The final (controversial) speech of the play.

INTIMATE SCENE SUGGESTIONS
I.i. *Lucentio trades identities with his servant, Tranio, so he may be near Bianca, whom he loves.*
II.i. *The fireworks-filled first meeting of Kate and Petruccio.*

PUBLIC SCENE SUGGESTION
IV.v. *In front of the servants and minor characters, Kate and Petruccio's battle of wills is played out.*

Love's Labour's Lost (c. 1593)
Although *Love's Labour's Lost* may be the hardest play in the Shakespeare canon to read, it is delightfully easy to understand in performance. Just as in *Two Gentlemen of Verona*, the story is concerned with young men. King Ferdinand of Navarre and his three companions take a vow to forswear the company of women and go into celibate study. Anyone can guess that this is a vow they will be unable to keep when the Princess of France and three accompanying gentlewomen arrive for a state visit. Each man schemes to hide his broken vows from the others. The complexity of the language can make this all seem obscure on the page, but it is hilariously clear in the theater.

The play ends with the four pairs of lovers about to be united, when unexpected news arrives that the Princess' father has died, making her Queen. She and her gentlewomen, who have all along shown far more maturity than the men, delay the marriages for at least a year to show proper mourning, and challenge the men to show themselves less foolish than they have appeared to date. For this reason, love's labors are lost. Apparently there was a sequel to this play, as a contemporary reference and a bookseller's list both mention *Love's Labour's Won*, but this play is now lost.

In addition to the group of eight main characters, *Love's Labour's Lost* features a parade of minor characters who are charming and eccentric, making especially good material for "character" actors. *Love's Labour's Lost* also contains the highest concentration of rhyme of any play in the canon and provides good material for exercises concentrating on couplets and rhyming verse.

SONNETS FROM THE PLAY

IV.ii.98–111. Nathaniel (reading Biron's sonnet): "If love makes me forsworn, how shall I swear to love?"
IV.iii.22–37. King: "So sweet a kiss the golden sun gives not"
IV.iii.55–69. Longueville: "Did not the heavenly rhetoric of thine eye"
IV.iii.97–116. Dumaine: "On a day—alack the day"

MONOLOGUE SUGGESTIONS

I.ii.149–164. Don Armado: "I do affect the very ground, which is base"
 The fantastical Spaniard's prose hymn of love.
III.i.159–190. Biron: "And I, forsooth, in love—I, that have been love's whip"
 A cynical lord is shocked to find that he, too, is susceptible to love.
IV.iii.286–339. Biron: "Have at you, then, affection's men-at-arms"
 Biron's great defense of love.
V.ii.770–794. Princess (now Queen): "A time, methinks, too short to make a world without end bargain in"
 The new queen declines a proposal of marriage.

INTIMATE SCENE SUGGESTIONS

I.ii. *Don Armado reveals his love for a peasant girl to his unusually wise page, Mote.*
III.i. *Mote attempts to cheer his love-sick master.*
III.i. *Biron enlists the aid of the clown, Costard, to deliver a secret letter to his love.*

LARGE ENSEMBLE SCENE SUGGESTIONS

IV.iii. *The four men reveal themselves (one at a time) to be in love, and are each discovered and shamed by the others who have been hiding.*
V.ii. *The men (in disguise) woo the wrong ladies, as the women have deliberately dressed in each other's garments and masks to trick the men.*

A Midsummer Night's Dream (c. 1594)

This play, which celebrates the power of the imagination, is one of the few in the canon to spring wholly from Shakespeare's imagination, rather than from earlier source material. It has three elaborately interwoven plot lines: The first of these concerns the upcoming marriage of Theseus, ruler of Athens, to Hippolyta, ruler of the Amazons, as well as the confused courtship of two young couples in his kingdom. The second plot describes the preparation of a play to be presented to Theseus and his bride by a group of earnest, but not theatrically accomplished, tradesmen. The final, fantastical plot line consists of the activities of the inhabitants of the kingdom of fairies (especially its quarreling king and queen, Oberon and Titania, and the king's servant, a "puck" named Robin Goodfellow) and their interaction with the mortals from the two other plot lines.

A Midsummer Night's Dream is perhaps the most performed, and popular, of all Shakespeare's plays. It can be played as broad comedy but is more apt to have an erotic edge in contemporary production. The dreamlike quality suggested by the title sometimes emerges as an unsettling near-nightmare, full of strange transformations and illuminating self-discoveries.

The script contains a number of well-known scenes and monologues. Like the other early comedies, its verse tends to be regular, with only a couple of special concerns for the actor: First, the play contains a very high proportion of rhyming couplets. Second, the supernatural characters commonly speak lines that are eight, rather than ten, syllables long.

MONOLOGUE SUGGESTIONS

I.i.226–251. Helena: "How happy some o'er other some can be!"
Helena resents that the man she loves, loves another. She plans to win him back.

II.i.121–137. Titania: "Set your heart at rest"
The queen of the fairies defies her king.

II.i.148–174. Oberon: "My gentle puck, come hither."*
In a beautifully poetic passage, Oberon sends Puck to fetch an herb.

II.i.249–267. Oberon: "I know a bank where the wild thyme grows"
Oberon reveals to Puck his plan to use a love charm on the humans.

INTIMATE SCENE SUGGESTIONS

II.i. *Puck and a fairy discuss the quarrel between the king and queen of fairies, whom they serve.*

II.i. *Helena pursues Demetrius into the woods, but he spurns her advances.*

III.ii. *Oberon chastises his unruly servant, Puck.*

PUBLIC SCENE SUGGESTIONS
II.i. *Oberon and Titania encounter each other and, in front of their courtiers, quarrel over a changeling boy.*

MATERIAL FOR A LARGE ENSEMBLE
The final act of *A Midsummer Night's Dream,* including the play-within-the-play, can be performed as an almost free-standing piece. It is sure-fire comedy, and as such is superb material for class projects for young performers.

Early Comedies by Shakespeare's Contemporaries

As Shakespeare began his career around 1590, he was surely aware of the plays of two comic writers: the novelist and dramatist John Lyly, whose mythological allegories for the boy players had charmed Elizabeth's court; and the novelist and dramatist Robert Greene, who used his educated "university wit" to decorate lurid romantic stories to please both plebeian and courtly audiences. These two very different writers exemplify the two primary trends in the theater of 1590: the highly artificial style of the boy players in the private theaters, and the rowdier, crowd-pleasing style of the men's companies in the public theater. Shakespeare and his later contemporaries clearly learned both comic modes, and used them to build a more robust and complex comic drama in the later 1590s and the 1600s.

John Lyly (c. 1554–1606)
Although the works of Lyly are rarely revived in the modern theater, his sophisticated, allegorical comedies for the boy players were favorites with Elizabeth's court in the 1580s and early 1590s. These plays were performed indoors, in private theaters like the Blackfriars, and give us a fascinating idea of an elite Elizabethan culture. Lyly was famous for a mannered, flowery prose style known as "euphuism" (named after his influential novel, *Euphues*). Through mythological allusions and highly stylized scenes, Lyly's plays subtly poked fun at rumors and scandals at court.

Shakespeare was clearly influenced by Lyly's formal designs and witty scenes for child actors. The comic scenes between the braggart

Don Armado and his page Mote in *Love's Labour's Lost* are very similar to those between the braggart Sir Tophas and his page Epiton in Lyly's *Endimion*; the punishment of Falstaff by pinching in *The Merry Wives of Windsor* echoes the punishment of Corsites in *Endimion*; and the famous eavesdropping scene in *Love's Labour's Lost* employs a structure similar to a scene in Lyly's *Gallathea* in which three nymphs discover that each has been cherishing a secret, forbidden love. *A Midsummer Night's Dream* also has echoes of Lylian style in its formal patterns, its key roles for children, its songs, its rendering of moonlight (a key theme in *Endimion*), and even in Bottom's ass' head, similar to the ass' ears suffered by Lyly's king *Midas*. Actors who want to improve their rhetorical skills should work on achieving the graceful balance of Lyly's lines.

Endimion (c. 1588)
MONOLOGUE SUGGESTION
II.i. Endimion: "O fair Cynthia! o unfortunate Endimion!"
> *Endimion swears that he will do anything for love of Cynthia, goddess of the moon.*

SCENE SUGGESTION
III.iii. *The braggart Sir Tophas confides in his page, Epiton, that he is in love and exchanges his armor for the tools of a lover.*

Campaspe (c. 1584)
MONOLOGUE SUGGESTIONS
I.iii. Melippus: "I had never such ado to warn scholars to come before a king."
> *The chamberlain describes how he tried to persuade Plato,*
> *Aristotle, and Diogenes to appear before Alexander the Great.*

II.ii. Hephestion: "I cannot tell, Alexander, whether the report be more shameful to be heard"
> *His friend tells Alexander the Great that it is not appropriate for a*
> *king to be in love.*

III.v. Apelles: "Unfortunate Apelles, and therefore unfortunate because Apelles!"
> *The artist Apelles has fallen in love with his model, Campaspe, the*
> *beloved of Alexander the Great.*

IV.ii. Campaspe: "Campaspe, it is hard to judge whether thy choice be more unwise"

Campaspe considers her feelings toward her suitors: Apelles, the artist, and Alexander, the emperor.

Gallathea (c. 1585)
MONOLOGUE SUGGESTION
II.v. Phillida: "Poor Phillida, curse the time of thy birth"

Phillida, disguised as a boy, is now attracted to a boy and wonders how to approach him.

SCENE SUGGESTION
III.ii. *Phillida and Gallathea, each girls disguised as boys, try to express their attraction to each other without giving away their disguises.*

Robert Greene (1558–1592)
Robert Greene brought his classical Cambridge education to the public theaters of London and reshaped the genre of popular comedy. Greene was a prolific and popular writer, more famous for his thirty-six pamphlets and prose romances than for his half-dozen plays. Nonetheless, Greene died at a young age in painful circumstances, indigent and ill from a life of dissipation. During his last illness, Greene produced his *Groatsworth of Wit*, a pamphlet that repents his involvement in theater and wild life and then adds a final satirical note attacking a newcomer on the London playwrighting scene, William Shakespeare. This note gives us our first definite reference to Shakespeare's whereabouts after the seven "lost years." Shakespeare may have had the last laugh, however, for late in his own career Shakespeare adapted Greene's prose romance, *Pandosto*, into his play, *The Winter's Tale*.

Greene is best remembered for a handful of plays that established the genre of romantic comedy. Onto the classical pattern of the young man's efforts to win an unattainable young woman, Greene grafted the exotic elements of the prose romance (magic, passion, and chivalry) alongside the homely elements of the native English folk plays (pastoral settings and folk heroes). Through his lyrical diction, Greene creates a comic world somewhere in between the pastoral vision of Arcadia and the spontaneous fun of a folk festival, which anticipates the "green world" of Shakespeare's festive comedies, such as *As You Like It* and *A Midsummer Night's Dream*.

Among Greene's best plays is *Friar Bacon and Friar Bungay*, which combines a pastoral romance between the beautiful milkmaid Margaret and the courtier Lacy, with dueling friar–magicians and regal pageantry. Its sophisticated double-plot structure is the first of its kind.

In *James IV*, Greene adapts an Italian story about a lustful young king and his virtuous, resourceful bride into one of the first real English tragicomedies. Greene's regular iambic pentameter flows quickly, and though the classical references may seem overly precious for milkmaids and country clowns, the overall effect should be one of natural grace and lyrical balance.

Friar Bacon and Friar Bungay (c.1589)
MONOLOGUE SUGGESTIONS
Scene 8. Margaret: "'Twas I, my lord, not Lacy stepped awry."
Margaret begs the Prince to blame her, not Lacy, for their forbidden love.
Scene 11. Friar Bacon: "Miles, thou knowest that I have dived into hell"
The magician impresses on his servant the importance of the night's work.
Scene 11. Friar Bacon: "'Tis past, indeed. Ah, villain, time is past"*
Friar Bacon curses his lost chance and the failure of his magical project.
Scene 14. Margaret: "Ah, father, when harmony of heaven"
Margaret renounces worldly love and prepares to enter a convent.

INTIMATE SCENE SUGGESTIONS
Scene 8. *Prince Edward accuses Lacy of betraying his interest in Margaret.*
Scene 15. *A devil invites the foolish Miles to join him in hell.*

James IV
MONOLOGUE SUGGESTIONS
I.i. King of Scots: "Now am I free from sight of common eye"*
The young king decides to throw off his wife Dorothea to pursue the beautiful Ida.
II.ii. Bishop: "What, like the eagle then"
The Bishop warns the king to heed his councilors, not new flatterers.

V.ii. Ateukin: "What? Was I born to be the scorn of kin?"
Ateukin realizes he cannot fulfill his promise to the king.

INTIMATE SCENE SUGGESTIONS
I.i. *The king confides in Ateukin, the parasite, who promises to help him.*
II.i. *Ateukin tells Ida of the king's desire for her (the Countess, Ida's mother, is also present).*
II.ii. *Ateukin and King of Scots plot to murder the queen so the king may wed Ida.*
IV.iv. *The clown Nano comforts Dorothea, the queen, who has escaped in a boy's disguise.*

Mature Comedies by Shakespeare (1595–1600)

In the five years leading up to the year 1600, Shakespeare wrote a new type of comedy. Where his early plays had concentrated on mistiming and misunderstanding, the plays written in this portion of his career concentrate on real conflicts, which are resolved only after considerable tribulation. They contain more recognizably human characters and at times inject complex but subordinated social concerns.

These mature comedies require a different performing sensibility. More daring choices are called for in playing the roles. Deeper, more carefully examined readings are possible—indeed, necessary—if the emotional possibilities inherent in stories of displacement and separation are to be realized. There is often more genuine loss and grief in these plays than we have seen to date, and players can explore more mood changes and variations of tone. The predominant tone remains comedic, but there are more shades of color in these compositions than in the early plays.

Much Ado About Nothing (c. 1598)
With *Much Ado About Nothing*, Shakespeare takes a sudden turn back to prose; and less than ten percent of the lines in this play are rhymed. Clearly, Shakespeare's mind is now running in a new direction: the self-proclaimed villain, Don John, is a character type we have not seen before in the comedies. Until now, Shakespeare's comedies were matters of misalignment. In *Much Ado*, the malicious Don John tricks the play's leading character, Claudio, into believing his love, Hero, has been un-

faithful to him on the eve of their wedding. Claudio denounces Hero in an especially brutal scene at their wedding, an act that is forgivable only because he is still a callow youth. (We don't actually know his age, but he is almost always played as a teenager.) In the end, things work out because Don John's accomplices are captured, almost inadvertently, by the comic constabulary, and the plot is revealed.

This play is much darker and harder edged than the plays that have preceded it. Its resolution is less easily accomplished. The play's comic reputation, in fact, mostly lies with Beatrice and Benedick, the witty single friends of Hero and Claudio. The story of how these reluctant lovers are tricked into revealing their ardor for each other is technically the subplot, but because these older characters have more depth and substance than the leading characters, they have long been at the center of most productions.

Monologue Suggestions
II.i.209–239. Benedick: "O, she used me past the endurance of a block"*
> *Benedick protests too much against Beatrice.*

II.iii.8–31. Benedick: "I do much wonder that one man, seeing how much another man is a fool"
> *Benedick describes his ideal woman.*

III.i.108–117. Beatrice: "What fire is in mine ears? Can this be true?"
> *Overhearing a conversation, which is actually a set-up, Beatrice becomes convinced that Benedick would love her except for her excessive pride.*

Intimate Scene Suggestions
III.i. *In the scene that immediately precedes Beatrice's monologue (in the preceding selection), her friends Hero and Ursula fool her into believing that Benedick loves her.*

IV.i. *Circumstances force Beatrice to ask Benedick to kill his best friend as proof of his love for her.*

V.ii. *Beatrice and Benedick admit their love for one another, but their accustomed bickering seems likely to continue.*

Public Scene Suggestion
I.i.95–118. *Benedick gets the best of Beatrice in a battle of words, perhaps unfairly, while their friends look on.*

As You Like It (c. 1600)

At first glance *As You Like It* looks to be a simple pastoral play. It is much more sophisticated than it seems on its surface, however. The conventional structure artfully conceals deeper currents beneath a veneer of naïveté.

The plot consists of the story of Rosalind, a princess banished by her evil (and usurping) uncle. She flees in disguise as a boy, with her cousin Celia, into the forest of Arden, where she meets a former acquaintance, Orlando. He is also fleeing an injustice, in this case perpetrated by his older brother. They had met once before, at a wrestling match where they fell in love, a fact that he celebrates in verses pinned to trees. On re-meeting, however, he fails to see through her disguise. In the guise of her alter ego, Ganymede, Rosalind teaches Orlando how to woo her. It is in this scene—in which a girl, who is pretending to be a boy, pretends to be a girl—that the cleverness of the design becomes clear. (This is only complicated by the fact that a boy would have originally played the girl playing a boy playing a girl.) The complexity of this arrangement, juxtaposed against the simplicity of the conversation, permits the audience and the actors to enjoy the multiple levels of role playing and awareness.

The resolution of the play, in which the former villains repent their evil ways and turn their lands and goods over to the brothers they had dispossessed and Rosalind reveals herself to Orlando, is intentionally artificial. In production, it can be magical.

The play has a very high proportion of prose, but it is exceedingly poetic in tone if not metrically. It works best when the contrast between the corrupt court and the green world of the forest is heightened.

Monologue Suggestions

II.i.1–17. Duke Senior: "Now, my co-mates and brothers in exile"
The displaced Duke tries to find the best in his new circumstances.
II.vii.12–34. Jaques: "A fool. A fool! I met a fool i' the forest"
A confirmed cynic reports having encountered a jester where he least expected to see one.
III.ii.359–382. Rosalind: "Love is merely a madness"*
In disguise, Rosalind speaks her mind on the vagaries of love.
III.v.36–64. Rosalind: "And why I pray you? Who might be your mother"

Rosalind, playing Ganymede, lectures the proud shepherdess Phoebe on love.

III.v.105–136. Phoebe: "Know'st thou the youth that spoke to me erewhile?"*

Soon after Rosalind's speech (preceding), Phoebe reveals her interest in Ganymede!

INTIMATE SCENE SUGGESTIONS

I.iii. *Rosalind and Celia's joking conversation is interrupted by the Duke, with news that Rosalind is exiled. Celia decides that she, too, will leave.*

II.iii. *Faithful old Adam informs his master, Orlando, that there is a plot on his life and makes a plan to flee with him.*

III.ii. *The sophisticated jester, Touchstone, makes fun of the country bumpkin, Corin.*

III.ii. *Celia reports to Rosalind (now in disguise) that Orlando has come to the forest.*

III.ii. *In her disguise as Ganymede, Rosalind gets the unsuspecting Orlando to let her cure him of his lovesickness.*

IV.i. *Rosalind gives Orlando his wooing lesson.*

III.v; IV.iii. *In a pair of scenes, Rosalind/Ganymede tries to convince Phoebe to love Silvius, but Phoebe falls in love with her/him instead.*

Twelfth Night (c. 1600)

This play, with its story about a set of separated twins, one of whom immediately goes into a cross-gender disguise, employs familiar devices in new and innovative ways. The separated twins in this play are Sebastian and Viola, an identical brother and sister pair. The consequences of their separation are often comic (echoing *Errors*) but are more often threaded with a serious sense of loss. Shipwrecked and mourning her brother, who she thinks has drowned, Viola assumes her boy's disguise for safety, not for love. Nonetheless, she soon finds herself adoring her new employer, the lovelorn Duke Orsino, who pines for the Countess Olivia, who has retreated to mourn for her late brother. Viola is sent to woo Olivia for Orsino, with complicated results.

Twelfth Night has many light and festive elements, including the wonderful drunkard Sir Toby Belch and his eccentric friends. However, the play has many dark strains running through it that give it extraordinary texture. For example, consider the subplot surrounding the character Antonio, who believes himself rejected and be-trayed at the very moment everyone else is finding happiness. The antagonist of this piece, appropriately named Malvolio, is less an evil villain (like those of *As You Like It* or *Much Ado About Nothing*) than an obnoxious stuffed shirt, akin to the exaggerated characters of Ben Jonson, who was also writing comedies at this time. The darkest moment in the play comes in its final scene, when Malvolio refuses to join in the happy ending and stamps away, angrily declaring he will be revenged on his opponents.

Although *Twelfth Night* has a good deal of prose, like the other romantic comedies of this period, it contains some of the most beau-tiful lyric speeches and songs of the canon and is full of poetically inclined scenes.

MONOLOGUE SUGGESTIONS
II.ii.15–39. Viola: "I left no ring with her. What means this lady?"
Viola discovers that the Lady Olivia has fallen in love with her dis-guised exterior.
III.i.129–126, 136–147. Olivia: "O world! How apt the poor are to be proud"*
Olivia declares her love for the reticent Cesario (Viola in disguise).
IV.iii. 1–35. Sebastian: "This is the air; that is the glorious sun"
Unaware of his disguised twin sister's groundwork, Sebastian finds himself suddenly beloved of the wealthy and beautiful Olivia.

INTIMATE SCENE SUGGESTIONS
I.iv. *Viola (in disguise as Cesario) is hired as a servant to the Duke of Illyria.*
II.iv. *The Duke sends Cesario/Viola to woo Olivia, but Viola loves the Duke herself.*
II.v. *The Countess Olivia rejects the message in favor of the messenger.*
III.i. *Olivia declares her love for Cesario/Viola, who is forced to reject her.*
III.i. *Viola discusses the oddities of fate with the jester Feste.*
IV.ii. *The jester Feste disguises himself as a lunatic curate to taunt the imprisoned Malvolio.*

The Merry Wives of Windsor (c. 1597)
The anomalous *The Merry Wives of Windsor* is the only one of Shakespeare's comedies to set middle-class characters in a simple en-vironment of his own time and his own country. In many ways, the

play resembles the domestic English comedies of his contemporaries, Dekker, Jonson, and Middleton. It is also almost entirely in prose.

The Merry Wives of Windsor shares several characters with the history plays, Henry IV, Parts 1 & 2, and Henry V, although their personalities differ in some regards. No one is sure whether The Merry Wives of Windsor precedes or follows the histories, so the direction of borrowing is not clear.

The Merry Wives of Windsor tells the story of Sir John Falstaff's attempts to seduce several married women of Windsor, completely without success. The comedy is generally broad. Legend has it that the play was composed on short notice (allegedly when Queen Elizabeth desired to see a play about Falstaff in love), which may account for its difference from other comedies in the canon. The location and other specific references in the play make it seem that it was written for a specific occasion, perhaps the induction of Shakespeare's patron into the Order of the Garter in 1597.

Monologue Suggestions

II.i.1–27. Mistress Page: "What, have I scaped love-letters in the holiday time of my beauty"
   Mistress Page unexpectedly receives a love letter from Falstaff.
II.ii.253–274. Ford: "What a damned Epicurean rascal is this!"
   Thinking his wife is meeting Falstaff, Ford goes into a jealous fit.

Intimate Scene Suggestions

II.i. *Mistress Ford and Mistress Page realize that Falstaff has sent them both the same love letter.*
II.ii. *In disguise, Ford hires Falstaff to test his wife's fidelity.*
III.iii. *Mistress Ford and Mistress Page get even with Falstaff.*
III.v. *Falstaff reports to the still-disguised Ford about the progress of his adventures.*

Mature Comedies by Shakespeare's Contemporaries: Jonson and Citizen Comedy

One literary approach to Elizabethan and Jacobean comedy has been to classify plays as "Shakespearean" or "Jonsonian," after Shakespeare's formidable colleague, Ben Jonson. In this system, Shakespearean comedy is "romantic," "festive," and "redemptive," while Jonsonian comedy is "satirical," "neoclassical," and "punitive." Since we have already seen that Shakespeare wrote many different styles of comedy, this theoretical model may not be especially helpful, but it does assert the importance of Jonson and his influence. Jonson made the classical comic tradition his own by employing its complicated plots of intrigue (usually involving trickery and disguise), its compact time scheme, and its ruthless representation of human folly. However, unlike the Roman writers, he set many of his plays in his own city, London, bringing his mocking gaze to subjects close to home.

The "citizen comedies" by Jonson and his contemporaries deal with the realistic problems of life in London. Although the scheming plots are filled with improbable coincidences, they are far more plausible than the fairytale conceits of Greene and Lyly. Money, social connections, and sex motivate the characters more often than the romantic concerns of true love and honor. Frequent references to local landmarks and events increase the sense of realism, and scenes are set in familiar shops, taverns, and markets. The London tapsters, whores, and apprentices speak in the slang expressions of their time (sometimes baffling the modern reader). The presumption of comic realism may have been dangerous to the playwrights; Jonson, Marston, Chapman, and Massinger were all imprisoned at one time or another for offending the political sensibilities of the authorities. Citizen comedy persisted, however, and continued into the eighteenth and nineteenth centuries.

Ben Jonson (1572–1637)

The brilliant, quarrelsome Ben Jonson assured his immortality with his energetic self-promotion alongside his prolific output of poetry, plays, and entertainments. Jonson studied the classics at Westminster School but never attended university. Instead, he served as an apprentice bricklayer, then as a mercenary soldier, and finally as an actor (infamous for killing another actor in a duel). Yet Jonson rose to become the foremost man of letters of his day and received honorary degrees from both Cambridge and Oxford, as well as a royal pension from the king.

Jonson began writing plays in collaboration with other dramatists. An early project with Thomas Nashe, *The Isle of Dogs* (1597), proved so subversive that the Privy Council imprisoned Jonson, destroyed the script, and temporarily closed the London theaters. Despite this inauspicious beginning, Jonson continued to collaborate with Thomas Dekker, Henry Chettle, Henry Porter, and John Marston. Relations among these competitive dramatists were often tense; Jonson's satires of Dekker and Marston, and theirs of him, fueled the so-called War of the Theatres of 1599–1601. His stormy collaborations with designer Inigo Jones brought Jonson his greatest successes at the court of James I, where they produced elaborate court entertainments, called "masques." (Shakespeare's late play, *The Tempest*, contains a masque in the fourth act.) Jonson's mythological scenarios and Jones' opulent designs, many of which are still extant, demonstrate the fantastic luxury of these elite entertainments.

Jonson is most famous for the plays he wrote independently. Unlike Shakespeare, Jonson wrote for various companies of players. *Every Man in His Humour* (1598) and *Every Man out of His Humour* (1599), played by the Lord Chamberlain's Men, established Jonson's reputation as a wit and a satirist. Jonson's characters are often motivated by one passion or obsession, called a "humour," which drives them through elaborate tricks and schemes. These exaggerated character types may not have psychological depth, but they can be hilarious in performance. Most of the characters in *Volpone*, Jonson's best-known play, are associated with animals; the foxy Volpone, who pretends to be on his deathbed, and his servant Mosca ("the Fly") dupe the "birds of prey" characters into giving up their wealth. The aptly named Truewit tricks Morose into marrying a surprising bride in *Epicoene, or the Silent Woman*. The small-time swindlers of *The Alchemist* cheat their clients into thinking they can turn base metals into gold. A vast array of London characters of all social classes and types interact at *Bartholomew Fair*, in a world temporarily without restraint.

Jonson scrupulously oversaw the publication of his work. One of his greatest achievements was to envision the collected *Works of Benjamin Jonson*, published in folio in 1613 under his direct supervision. This was the first such volume in history, and it gave printed drama new legitimacy as literature. His volume was certainly the inspiration for Hemmings and Condell to produce a similar book collecting the works of their colleague, Shakespeare, a decade later.

Although Jonson wrote two classically based tragedies, *Sejanus* and *Catiline*, actors now are more likely to encounter his satirical comedies. Jonson asserted that it was "the office of a comic poet to imitate justice, and instruct to life," that is, that comedy should expose and punish the vices and follies of society in order to teach a lesson. Jonson's comic characters are not on a journey toward greater maturity and self-knowledge, as Shakespeare's often are, and the plays end more often with their castigation than their redemption.

Try to commit absolutely to the characters' greedy and self-advancing schemes. You can fuel these outrageous objectives by using the succulent, feverish language that Jonson provides. The verbal energy is contagious and signals not only the characters' rapid imagination, but also the urgency of the farcical action. But don't forget to do your homework— seventeenth-century slang abounds in these plays.

Every Man in His Humour (1598)
MONOLOGUE SUGGESTION

II.v. Knowell: "I cannot lose the thought, yet, of this letter"
Knowell (a role that Shakespeare probably played) laments that children aren't raised properly anymore.

Every Man out of His Humour (1599)
MONOLOGUE SUGGESTIONS

I.i. Carlo Buffone: "First, to be an accomplished gentleman"*
The jester describes the qualities of gentlemen.
IV.iv. Fastidious Brisk: "Good faith, signior, now you speak of a quarrel"*
The dandy describes the damage done to his clothes in a recent duel.

Volpone (1606)
MONOLOGUE SUGGESTIONS

III.i. Mosca: "I fear I shall begin to grow in love"
Mosca revels in the life of a parasite.
III.iv. Lady Would-be: "I thank you, good sir. Pray you signify"*
Lady Would-be frets to her maids over her appearance.
III.vii. Celia: "If you have ears that will be pierced, or eyes"
Celia begs Volpone not to ravish her.

INTIMATE SCENE SUGGESTIONS

I.iii. *Volpone and his parasitic servant, Mosca, trick suspicious Voltore out of a gift, to ensure a place in the "dying" Volpone's will.*
II.vi. *Mosca tricks Corvino into supplying his young wife for Volpone's enjoyment.*

Epicoene, or The Silent Woman (1609)
MONOLOGUE SUGGESTIONS

I.i. Truewit: "I love a good dressing before any beauty o'the world."*
   Truewit applauds the secret skills of a lady's toilette.

II.i. La Foole: "They all come out of our house, the La Fooles of the north"
   La Foole tries to impress his fellows with his pedigree and his titled acquaintances.

II.ii. Truewit: "They say you are to marry; to marry!"*
   Truewit warns Morose of the dangers of marriage.

III.i. Mistress Otter: "By my integrity, I'll send you over to the Bankside"
   She forbids her henpecked husband to carouse with his friends at home.

IV.ii. Truewit: "A man should not doubt to overcome any woman."*
   The wit describes how men can vary their amorous strategies according to a woman's taste.

SCENE SUGGESTION
IV.v. *Truewit tricks Sir Amorous La Foole into hiding from a supposed enemy.*

The Alchemist (1610)
MONOLOGUE SUGGESTIONS

I.i. Dol Common: "O me! We are ruined! Lost!"*
   Dol curses her squabbling partners in crime.

II.ii. Sir Epicure Mammon: "Lungs, I will set a period"*
   A hedonist's erotic fantasy of what alchemy will provide.

Bartholomew Fair (1614)
MONOLOGUE SUGGESTION

II.ii. Ursula: "Fie upon't! Who would wear out their youth and prime thus in roasting of pigs"*
   The enormous Ursula calls for beer to cool herself off.

Thomas Dekker (c. 1572–1632)
Dekker was primarily a collaborator who wrote acts and scenes to order, on subjects not necessarily of his own choosing, often for Philip Henslowe and the Lord Admiral's Men. Because of these joint efforts, Dekker's bibliography is tangled, but he seems to have had a hand in more than forty plays, of which about twenty survive. Dekker had a keen eye for the daily life of his home city, London,

which he put to good use in his prose works as well as his plays; two famous pamphlets, *The Gull's Handbook* and *The Seven Deadly Sins of London,* provide a window into the popular culture of the city. Three plays he co-wrote with Middleton, the two parts of *The Honest Whore* and *The Roaring Girl,* have recently aroused interest because of their proto-feminist subject matter. Dekker was also one of the parties in the "War of the Theatres," a battle of words that teamed him with John Marston against Ben Jonson in an exchange of satirical plays in which each side parodied the other on stage and in print. Yet Dekker's particular genius was not satire, but a vivacious romantic comedy, which often included songs, dances, and special effects to amuse his audience.

Dekker's best-known comedy, *The Shoemakers' Holiday*, is a delightful urban romance of disguised lovers under the protection of Simon Eyre, the jolly shoemaker who becomes the Lord Mayor of London. It contains wonderful ensemble scenes and festive songs. The two parts of *The Honest Whore*, co-authored with Middleton, show the influence of the morality plays on these "comedies" about the reformation of Bellafront, the title character, and the economic circumstances that tempt her to resume her former trade. (A much later play, *The Witch of Edmonton*, co-authored with William Rowley and John Ford, redirected Dekker's romantic sense into dark tragicomedy. Scenes from it are included in chapter 4 of this book.)

The Shoemakers' Holiday (1599)
MONOLOGUE SUGGESTIONS
I.ii. Sybil: "By my troth, I scant knew him"*
   Sybil describes seeing her friend's lover at court.
V.i. Eyre: "Go! Vanish! Vanish! Avaunt, I say!"
   The shoemaker relishes his new role as Lord Mayor.

INTIMATE SCENE SUGGESTION
III.iv. *Hammon tells Jane that her husband has been killed and then tries to seduce her.*

The Honest Whore (Part 1, 1604; Part 2, c. 1605)
MONOLOGUE SUGGESTIONS
Part 1, I.i. Hippolito: "Curst be that day for ever that robbed her"
   Hippolito mourns his beloved Infelice, who has (supposedly) died recently.

Part 1, II.i. Bellafront: "Curst be that minute—for it was no more"
Bellafront berates herself for her sins and determines to change.

Part 1, IV.i. Hippolito: "My Infelice's face, her brow, her eye"
Gazing first on his late fiancee's picture and then on a skull, Hippolito thinks about mortality and the foolish concerns of the living.

Part 2, IV.i. Bellafront: "To prove a woman should not be a whore"
In several long speeches in rhyming couplets, Bellafront refutes her former profession.

SCENE SUGGESTIONS

Part 1, I.ii. *Viola convinces her brother Fustigo to help her make her husband jealous.*

Part 1, II.i. *Hippolito describes to Bellafront why she is damned for being a whore, and she decides to reform to win his affection.*

Part 1, IV.iv. *The Doctor amazes Hippolito with the news that Infelice is actually alive and waiting to marry him.*

Part 2, I.ii. *Hippolito tells the old Orlando Friscobaldo that his disowned daughter Bellafront is now married but living in poverty while her husband is in jail.*

Part 2, II.i. *Orlando Friscobaldo, under the guise of the servant Pacheco, hears evidence of his daughter Bellafront's reformation and remorse.*

Part 2, III.i. *Orlando, still in servant's disguise, gives to Infelice the letter, purse, and ring that her husband Hippolito had used unsuccessfully to seduce Bellafront.*

Part 2, III.i. *Infelice toys with her husband Hippolito before revealing the evidence of his infidelity.*

Thomas Middleton (1580–1627)

Londoner Thomas Middleton attended Oxford, but left without a degree, and became one of the leading playwrights in the generation after Shakespeare. In 1602, Middleton began his career in Philip Henslowe's stable of writers, but within a few years, he was writing independent comedies for the boys' companies that established his reputation as a satirist. *A Mad World, My Masters, Michaelmas Term,* and *A Trick to Catch the Old One* (all 1605–1607) fill quick-moving intrigue plots of tricks and disguises with comic characters from the streets of London: spendthrift young men, wealthy uncles, courtesans, Puritans, money-lenders, adulterers, and con artists. Although these comic characters are similar to those of Jonson's plays, Middleton takes a more ironic attitude toward his sinful characters, and presents their crimes with good humor rather than moral outrage. A slightly later play, *A Chaste Maid in Cheapside* (1613), is one of the masterpieces of "citizen comedy," in which almost every character schemes to prevent the arranged marriage between Moll Yellowhammer, the goldsmith's daughter, and the wealthy Sir Walter Whorehound, who for ten years has supported his mistress, Mrs. Allwit, her contented husband, and their large family.

During the 1610s and 1620s, Middleton's satire grew darker, and he began to write tragicomedies and tragedies. Some of these plays are included in chapter 2.

Middleton also wrote a number of civic pageants and entertainments and was given the honorary title (and stipend) of City Chronologer in 1620. With his long career, prolific and diverse accomplishments, and civic honors, Middleton is truly one of the theatrical giants of the Jacobean period. Interestingly, his very theatricality has kept him out of later scholarship. Middleton's work is not particularly satisfying as poetry, and most of his plays have therefore been omitted from literary collections. However, Middleton's genius for rapid action, pithy characterization, and complex layers of connecting relationships quickly becomes apparent in performance, and his scenes are well worth investigating. Keep in mind that Middleton's ironic wit sharpens even the darkest situations, and that the tricksters and con artists of the comedies are driven by very strong and selfish motivations.

A Mad World, My Masters (c.1605)
MONOLOGUE SUGGESTIONS
I.i. Mother: "Every part of the world shoots up daily into more subtlety."
> *The devious mother describes how she advertises her daughter's "virginity" to make money.*
IV.i. Master Penitent Brothel: "Ha! Read that place again."
> *Master Penitent regrets his adulterous affair with Mistress Harebrain and fears damnation.*

A Chaste Maid in Cheapside (1613)
MONOLOGUE SUGGESTIONS
I.i. Maudline: "You are a dull maid alate."*
> *Maudline scolds her daughter for her gloomy behavior, which won't catch a husband.*

I.ii. Allwit: "The founder's come to town."
Allwit cheerfully describes how his wife's lover, Sir Walter Whorehound, pays all the family expenses.

II.i. Touchwood Senior: "But, as thou say'st, we must give way to need"*
Touchwood and his wife agree to separate temporarily to avoid the expense of more children.

IV.i. Tim: "I mar'l what this gentlewoman should be"
The foolish Tim wonders about the bride his parents have arranged for him.

Thomas Heywood (1574–1641)

In 1633, Heywood remarked that he had had "an entire hand, or at least a main finger" in the composition of 220 plays. He also found time to write poetry, translations, pageants, religious tracts, and a famous pamphlet, *An Apology for Actors* (1612), which defended the theater from Puritan attacks. This astonishing output reminds us of the circumstances in which the dramatists wrote: they wrote quickly, in teams, and effectively recycled successful bits for the actors and companies they knew. Heywood, like so many other playwrights, began his career writing to order for Henslowe and the Admiral's Men. Like Shakespeare, Heywood was also an actor and a shareholder in a company (the Earl of Worcester's Men, later the Queen Anne's Men).

Although many have been lost, we have plays from Heywood in every genre, from classical tragedies such as *The Rape of Lucrece*, to English history plays such as *Edward IV* and *If You Know Not Me, You Know Nobody*, to mythological dramas such as *The Golden Age*, to popular comedies such as *The Wise Woman of Hogsdon*. Heywood's masterpiece is *A Woman Killed with Kindness*, a domestic tragedy about an ordinary English family (selections appear in chapter 2). Heywood seems to have had a keen sense of what would be popular with the London audiences in the public theaters. *The Fair Maid of the West*, one of his most successful plays, follows the Indiana Jones–style adventures of Bess Bridges, a resourceful barmaid, who takes to the high seas and outwits the King of Fez to win her sweetheart, Spencer. The exciting action proved so popular that many years later, Heywood wrote a second part to the play.

The Fair Maid of the West (Part 1, c.1600; Part 2, c. 1630)
MONOLOGUE SUGGESTIONS

Part 2, III.ii. Bess: "Prize you my love no better than to rate it"*
  When Spencer prepares to leave for a debt to his honor, Bess accuses him of betrayal.
Part 2, IV.ii. Clem: "Where are my bashaws now?"
  Shipwrecked in Florence, Clem plans to return to his old trade of drawing wine.

SCENE SUGGESTIONS

Part 1, II.iii. *In her male disguise, Bess challenges the cowardly braggart Roughman.*
Part 1, III.iv. *Bess discovers that Goodlack is the trusted friend of her beloved Spencer and asks him to buy a ship for her command.*
Part 2, I.i. *Tota, the Queen of Fez, bribes Roughman to betray his captain Spencer.*
Part 2, I.i. *Mullisheg, the King of Fez, bribes Goodlack to bring Bess to his bed.*
Part 2, I.i. *Roughman and Goodlack compare their charges, and agree to double-cross the King and Queen.*
Part 2, V.ii. *Spencer finds Bess asleep but has sworn to his new master not to touch her.*

Problem Plays and Satires by Shakespeare (1600–1606)

At the time when he was writing the great tragedies, Shakespeare also wrote several comedies that have come to be known as "problem plays." These are plays that, for various reasons, are hard to reconcile with their classification as comedies. Comedies, by their simplest definition, end "happily," with conflicts resolved and social order restored. Yet *The Merchant of Venice* contains unresolved issues of race and cultural relations that make its happy ending hard to accept at face value. *Troilus and Cressida* ends unhappily. *Measure for Measure* ends ambiguously, allowing diametrically opposed resolutions in different productions. *All's Well That Ends Well* has a written reconciliation, but the events that have come before it undermine any "happily ever after" certainty and leave the characters and the audience with only a tentative sense of resolution. Though many of these resolutions may have been less problematic in the seventeenth century than they have become in the twentieth, these plays are undoubtedly more complex than the earlier comedies. They also contain complicated issues and challenging verbal constructions, which can make them "problems" for audiences in the twentieth century.

The three later "problem comedies" focus on problems of class, problems of gender, and, particularly, problems arising out of human sexuality. They are dark, personal plays, with much thematically in common with the Sonnets. In contemporary production all three have proven to be capable of enthralling and invigorating audiences, but none of them can be considered a knee-slapping good time. They are thought, rather than laughter, provoking.

The Merchant of Venice

The plot of *The Merchant of Venice* derives from traditional tales and is meant to function as romantic comedy. In it, a young Venetian named Bassanio hopes to marry a wealthy young heiress, Portia. She, however, can be married only to the man who passes a test devised by her late father, in which suitors choose from among three "caskets."

Bassanio is short of cash for the trip to Belmont to pursue Portia, so he borrows money from his friend Antonio, the merchant of the title. Since Antonio does not have ready cash, he in turn borrows the money from the Jewish moneylender, Shylock. Because of old animosity, the moneylender agrees only on the fairytale condition that in case of forfeiture he be repaid with a pound of Antonio's flesh.

Bassanio, in the way of romantic comedy, successfully chooses the correct casket and marries Portia. Back in Venice, Antonio's trading ventures turn sour and he is unable to repay his loan, so Shylock demands his pound of flesh. The matter goes to trial, where the law sides with Shylock until Portia (in cross-gender disguise) saves the day with some legal quibbles that turn Shylock's insistence on the letter of the law against him. He is forced to concede the cause, is forcibly taught generosity and mercifulness, and is made a more homogeneous member of the community by being sentenced to embrace Christian values.

Defending and redeeming *The Merchant of Venice* is no easy task in our post-Holocaust, multiracial age, where the plea that "this is just a folk story" can't override concerns about intolerance. There are, after all, unmistakably racist and anti-semitic statements un-abashedly uttered in the play. For this reason, *Merchant* has become a problem play in our time. It is extremely difficult to accept as a romantic comedy, and there is not enough exposure of hypocrisy for it to function as a satire or morality play. The "happy" ending of the subplot, where Shylock "learns" the values of generosity and mercy, lurks on the edges of tragedy for our time, and threatens to unbalance the whole piece.

Because of these problems, *Merchant* is easier to deal with in scene study than in production. It has a great deal of extractable material, but it is nonetheless wise to think through the full roles carefully before approaching them. The problems presented by the play cannot be easily excused or ignored.

MONOLOGUE SUGGESTIONS

I.iii.102–124. Shylock: "Signior Antonio, many a time and oft"
   The moneylender confronts the would-be borrower about his past abuses.
III.ii.149–174. Portia: "You see, my Lord Bassanio, where I stand"
   Now that he has passed the casket test, Portia pledges herself to Bassanio.

INTIMATE SCENE SUGGESTIONS

I.i. *Bassanio seeks funds from his friend Antonio to pursue the wealthy Portia.*
I.ii. *The wealthy Portia reviews the list of her suitors with her maid, Nerissa.*
I.iii. *Though Bassanio has misgivings, Antonio agrees to the bizarre terms of Shylock's loan.*
II.ii. *When he comes to visit, Launcelot teases his blind and confused father, Old Gobbo.*
III.ii. *While Portia watches tensely, Bassanio passes the casket test.*
V.ii. *The newlyweds Jessica and Lorenzo celebrate the beauty of the night.*

Troilus and Cressida

The names of the tragic lovers Troilus and Cressida were once as well known as those of Romeo and Juliet; so the play's title does not suggest comedy, nor does much of its action. In fact, the comedy of the play mostly derives from just two characters, Cressida's uncle

Pandarus in the Trojan scenes and the cynical Thersytes in the Greek ones.

The plot is, on one level, the intimate story of the rise and fall of the naive Troilus' love affair with Cressida, which is contrasted against the larger progress of the Trojan War. Greeks and Trojans alike are worn down by the war that has long since quit making sense.

It is the odd mixture of tragic, comic, philosophic, and satiric elements that have made this play problematic. At times, it seems to celebrate martial values, but more often it satirizes them. In places, it seems to wallow in romance, but more often it takes a rather cynical view of sexual appetites.

The poetry and language of the play are dense and, at times, quite beautiful. The extractable material from this play is more often serious in tone than comic, but because of the play's relative obscurity in the canon, there is much fresh audition and scene study material available from it.

Monologue Suggestions

Prologue.1–31. "In Troy there lies the scene."
  A chorus figure sets the scene.
I.i.45–60. Troilus: "O Pandarus! I tell thee, Pandarus"
  Romeo-like, Troilus is completely smitten.
II.ii.8–24. Hector: "Though no man lesser fears the Greeks than I"
  The Trojan hero argues that Helen is not worth a war.
II.iii.1–19. Thersites: "How now, Troilus?"
  The bitter, funny railing of Thersites.
III.ii.102–122. Cressida: "Boldness comes to me now, and brings me heart"*
  Cressida confesses her love for Troilus.
V.ii.138–160. Troilus: "If beauty have a soul, this is not she."
  Unable to believe what he is seeing, Troilus falls apart when he sees Cressida with Diomedes.

Intimate Scene Suggestions

I.i. *Pandarus subtly and cynically encourages Troilus' infatuation with Cressida.*
I.ii. *Cressida tries to seem indifferent with Pandarus as he praises Troilus, but fails.*

I.iii. *Ulysses and Nestor scheme to get the totally indifferent Achilles into battle.*

III.ii. *Brought together by Pandarus, Troilus and Cressida pledge their love.*

III.iv. *Ulysses and Achilles discuss fame.*

Measure for Measure

Written as much as fifteen years after Shakespeare's earliest comedies, *Measure for Measure* stretches the limits of the comic form nearly as far as they can go. The play's central action is the attempt of Isabella, a young novice on the verge of taking her vows to become a nun, to argue on behalf of her brother, Claudio, who has been sentenced to death for breaking the vice laws by impregnating his fiancée. The judge who has imposed this harsh sentence is a Puritan deputizing for Vienna's Duke Vincentio, who is said to be traveling, but is in fact in disguise nearby. The judge, with the ironic name of Angelo, proves to be corrupt. He proposes to Isabella that she should sleep with him in exchange for her brother's life. Unbeknownst to him, another woman (his former fiancée) is substituted in the dark bed, but Angelo orders Claudio's death nonetheless.

This play seems to veer toward tragedy at almost every turn. The direst consequences are averted only because the Duke intervenes and saves the young man's life. He removes Angelo from office and punishes him. He even offers the opportunity for a fairytale happy ending, by proposing marriage to Isabella. The play ends extremely ambiguously, however, because the would-be nun does not speak. It is a matter for every production to decide whether she accepts or declines or whether the matter is left unresolved.

Like *Troilus and Cressida*, this play has much exciting, extractable material that is serious in tone. The comedy in *Measure for Measure* is muted, so most of the following monologues and scenes are suggested with the caveat that they are generally less appropriate for work centering on comic technique.

MONOLOGUE SUGGESTIONS

II.iv.1–17. Angelo: "When I would pray and think, I think and pray"
   Unable to pray, the anguished Angelo decides to follow his worst instincts.

II.iv.171–187. Isabella: "To whom should I complain?"
Isabella realizes that no one will believe she has been propositioned by a corrupt judge. She rationalizes that her brother would rather die than have her sleep with the judge.

III.i.5–41. Duke: "Be absolute for death."
Disguised as a friar, the Duke preaches a sermon of acceptance of one's mortality.

III.i.118–132. Claudio: "Ay, but to die, and go we know not where"
Claudio, honestly and movingly, expresses his fear of dying.

INTIMATE SCENE SUGGESTIONS

I.iv. *The scoundrel Lucio finds Isabella in the nunnery to inform her that her brother is in danger.*

II.ii. *With Lucio looking on, Isabella begs the judge, Angelo, for her condemned brother's life.*

II.v. *Angelo proposes to spare Claudio if Isabella will sleep with him.*

III.i. *Isabella asks her brother, Claudio, to accept his fate so as to spare her virtue.*

III.ii. *Lucio feels free to libel the Duke to a friar, not realizing it is the Duke in disguise.*

IV.ii. *The Duke and the Provost cook up a plan to save Claudio's life.*

All's Well That Ends Well

Many of Shakespeare's plays that center especially strongly on women have had trouble finding a steady place in the repertoire, because until recently (when women began to occupy producer and artistic director positions) they had no champions. *All's Well That Ends Well* seems to have suffered from this more than any other play. The central character of the play is Helen, a physician's daughter of grace and intellect but without social rank. She loves Bertram, the noble son of the household in which she lives, but he refuses to consider her because she is so far below him.

Helen magically cures the King of a mysterious disease, and in gratitude the King grants her the husband of her choice, which is, of course, Bertram. He objects but is married to Helen against his will. He immediately rebels by leaving for the Italian war with his best friend Parolles, a liar and coward, thereby abandoning his wife. He swears that he will not return until she finds herself pregnant by him, presumably an impossibility. In Italy, Bertram proves valiant on the battlefield, but juvenile off of it, where he seeks to seduce an innocent young woman named Diana. Helen travels to Italy and substitutes herself for Diana in a bedtrick that echoes, but reverses, the one used in *Measure for Measure*.

Helen undergoes a series of trials, wins a husband, and ultimately redeems him in an almost religious metaphor. It is a story that we know extremely well from countless folk stories, only we are not used to seeing it in this gender-reversed form. Only recently have feminist scholars begun to reveal the power of the central character and the play as a whole, which contains especially strong pieces for women. Not only is Helen's role remarkably rewarding, but the part of Bertram's mother, the Countess, was said by Bernard Shaw to be "the most beautiful old woman's part ever written."

MONOLOGUE SUGGESTIONS
I.i.105–151. Parolles: "Are you meditating on virginity?"*
Extractable from the scene (following) is this off-color but hilarious tirade.
I.i.74–94. Helen: "I think not on my father"
Because she loves Bertram, who is impossibly far above her in station, Helen weeps.
I.iii.175–201. Helen: "Then I confess/Here on my knee, before high heaven and you"
To the Countess, Helen admits she loves Bertram.
III.ii.99–129. Helen: "Till I have no wife I have nothing in France."
Helen decides to leave France so that her husband will return from the war that endangers him.

INTIMATE SCENE SUGGESTIONS
I.i. *Helen and Parolles, in a remarkably frank discussion, banter about virginity.*
I.iii. *The Countess encourages Helen's love for her son.*
III.vii. *With the help of a widow, Helen hatches a plan to recapture her husband.*

PUBLIC SCENE SUGGESTION
II.v. *In front of his friend and servants, Helen humbles herself to beg a kiss of her new husband in hopes of enticing him home, but he has other ideas.*

Problem Plays and Satires by Shakespeare's Contemporaries

Although satire was technically illegal, it was flourishing on the English stage by the accession of King James in 1603. Satire typically mocks the wickedness or follies of society by ridiculing characters who demonstrate contemptible flaws. While the civil authorities found it very funny to see the failings of Italy and Spain satirized on the stage, they did not care to see themselves in such an unflattering guise, which explains why so many plays of this period have foreign settings.

Ben Jonson's vigorous satirical comedies took ordinary citizens to task for their greed, hypocrisy, and vanity. His colleague John Marston moved into more dangerous territory with satirical representations of corrupt courts and courtiers. Marston's plays often employ a disguised outsider to observe and comment on the failings of the court. Such characters recur throughout Jacobean drama and are often referred to as "malcontents," after Marston's play by that name. The function of these satirical critics, who seek to reform corruption and restore order, comes close to that of the revenger in tragedy, who often assumes a disguise to infiltrate a decadent court (as in *The Revenger's Tragedy*). We can see this relationship not only in the dark comedies of Marston and his contemporaries, but also in the Jacobean revenge tragedies, which blend grotesque crimes with a horrible sense of humor.

For actors, this blend of tragic and comic may be disconcerting at first. However, it provides wonderful material for exploring very strong emotional motivations under the quicksilver diction of comedy.

John Marston (1576–1634)

John Marston was born to an Italian mother and an English father, a Coventry lawyer who installed his son as a law student at the Inns of Court after he completed his degree at Oxford. The elder Marston, like many anxious parents of theater students, hoped that his son would "foregoe his delighte in playes vayne studdyes and fooleryes." Nevertheless, Marston enjoyed a notable career as a playwright from about 1598 to 1608, but after his mysterious imprisonment in 1608, he gave up his ties to the theater and became a priest.

Literary critics have argued over the classification of Marston's satirical plays, with some of the same concerns as those brought to Shakespeare's "problem comedies": are they innocent or subversive, comedies or tragicomedies, failures or innovations? Marston seems to have known that his plays belonged to the stage rather than the page; in his introduction to the 1606 publication of *The Fawn*, he remarks that "Comedies are writ to be spoken, not read. Remember the life of these things consists in action." Indeed, Marston seems to be fascinated by theatricality, and the characters in his best plays famously assume disguises and put on new roles with which to observe and criticize a corrupt society.

In *The Malcontent*, Altofronto, the banished Duke of Genoa, assumes the role of the "malcontented" Malevole in order to return to his corrupt court, where he amuses the new Duke Pietro with his satirical barbs while he engineers his own restoration.

The Fawn (also known as *Parasitaster*) turns on a disguise plot much like that of Shakespeare's *Measure for Measure*. Hercules, the Duke of Ferrara, disguises himself as "Faunus" in order to observe the court of Urbino, where his son Tiberio is wooing princess Dulcimel, ostensibly for his father. Unlike the critical Malevole in *The Malcontent*, "Faunus" becomes the perfect courtier, flattering everyone's vanities and delusions.

Antonio and Mellida is an early tragicomedy written (as were most of Marston's plays) for a children's company, which gives its romantic elements a humorous cast. The play begins rather like *Twelfth Night*: on the seashore, Antonio grieves for his drowned father and assumes a woman's disguise in order to get close to his beloved Mellida. Although everyone is reunited by the end of this play, its popularity inspired Marston to write a more tragic sequel, *Antonio's Revenge*.

The Fawn (Parasitaster) (1604–1606)
MONOLOGUE SUGGESTIONS
I.i. Hercules: "And now, thou ceremonious sovereignty"
The Duke of Ferrara assumes the disguise of the flattering Faunus.
II.i. Zoya: "Is he gone? Is he blown off?"*
Donna Zoya explains that she has started false rumors of her pregnancy to annoy her husband.

II.i. Hercules: "As indeed, why should any woman only love any one man"

> In this satirical speech, "Faunus" suggests that women should have different lovers for different qualities.

III.i. Nymphadoro: "I'll tell thee: for mine own part, I am a perfect Ovidian"

> The courtier explains how he can love any woman for her particular charms.

IV.i. Puttota: "Never entreat me, never beseech me to have pity forsooth on your master"*

> The laundress soundly rejects the advances of Herod, the courtier.

IV.i. Zuccone: "I will have no mercy, I will not relent."*

> The duped husband rejects his wife Zoya, imagining that she has been unfaithful to him.

SCENE SUGGESTIONS

III.i. The princess Dulcimel confides in Philocalia that she intends to win the love of Tiberio without her father's consent.

IV.i. Zuccone realizes he has cast away his faithful wife Zoya and turns to "Faunus" for advice.

The Malcontent (1603–1604)
MONOLOGUE SUGGESTIONS

I.iii. Malevole: "O God, for a woman to make a man that which God never created"*

> Malevole encourages Duke Pietro to imagine how his wife has cuckolded him with Mendoza.

I.iii. Malevole: "Lean thoughtfulness, a sallow meditation"

> Using the "free speech" of his disguise, Malevole plans to take revenge on the Duke.

I.v. Mendoza: "Now, Good Elysium! what a delicious heaven it is for a man to be in a prince's favor!"

> Mendoza relishes the Duchess' favors and envies the privileges of the Duke.

II.i. Mendoza: "He's caught; the woodcock's head is in the noose."

> Mendoza plans to execute his revenge on the unsuspecting Duke, Duchess, and Ferneze.

III.ii. Malevole: "Thy young lady wife goes to Florence with thee too, does she not?"*

Malevole urges Bilioso not to leave his wife subject to the lascivious, decadent court.

SCENE SUGGESTION
II.v. *Mendoza and the Duchess Aurelia conspire to murder Duke Pietro, who suspects they have betrayed him.*

Antonio and Mellida (c. 1599)
MONOLOGUE SUGGESTIONS
I.i. Antonio: "Heart, wilt not break? And thou, my abhorred life"
   After a terrible sea battle, Antonio fears he has lost his father, Andrugio, and any hope of winning his beloved Mellida.
III.i. Andrugio: "My thoughts are fix'd in contemplation"
   The despairing Andrugio wishes the earth would pity and swallow him.
IV.i. Antonio: "Stop; stop Antonio; stay Antonio."
   In a new disguise, Antonio questions the relationship between the spirit and the corporal body.
IV.i. Andrugio: "Why man, I never was a prince till now."
   Andrugio has found new meaning in living simply in accordance with his own values.

Philip Massinger (1583–1640)
After growing up in a privileged Wiltshire family, Philip Massinger started his career in the theater around 1613, just as Shakespeare was retiring, and began collaborating with Shakespeare's former partner, John Fletcher. Twelve of the plays written jointly by Massinger and Fletcher were printed in the Beaumont and Fletcher folio of 1647, although Massinger was not credited. Just as Fletcher had inherited from Shakespeare his post as chief dramatist with the King's Men in 1616, Massinger in turn inherited the position from Fletcher in 1625, under the reign of Charles I. Despite this prestigious contract, Massinger seems never to have found the financial rewards he sought; in a letter to a potential patron, he dismissed his plays as "those toys I would not father," were it not for economic necessity.

Massinger contributed to more than fifty plays, most in the style of romantic tragicomedy associated with Fletcher, his partner and mentor. Many of them reveal Massinger's serious consideration of moral and political issues. However, he is best known for two comedies that held the English stage for centuries. David Garrick and Edmund Kean were only two of the many great actors to star in the role of Sir Giles Overreach, the tyrannical financier and social climber who strives to ruin his neighbors in *A New Way to Pay Old Debts*. The plot of *The City Madam*, a city comedy often revived in the eighteenth and nineteenth centuries, uses a plot device similar to that of Shakespeare's *Measure for Measure*. Sir John Frugal, who has overindulged his extravagant wife and daughters, gives control of the household to his outwardly humble brother, Luke. Luke soon reveals his hidden greed and lust for power, but by the end, he is caught and order is restored. In Massinger's sophisticated comic characters, who are obsessed with money and social position, we can see that drama and society have changed from Elizabethan exuberance to the more nervous materialism of the Caroline world. Massinger leads English comedy toward the great social satires that would evolve after the Restoration.

A New Way to Pay Old Debts (c. 1625)
SCENE SUGGESTIONS
I.i. *Young Allworth discusses his hopes for winning Margaret Overreach with his late father's prodigal friend, Wellborn.*
III.ii. *Sir Giles Overreach teaches his horrified daughter, Margaret, how to seduce Lord Lovell; Justice Greedy interrupts with plans for the seduction dinner.*

The City Madam (1632)
MONOLOGUE SUGGESTIONS
I.ii. Plenty: "What with me, sir!"*
   Mr. Plenty, a country gentleman, insists that he is just as good a suitor as Sir Maurice Lacy.
II.i. Luke: "Have you almost serv'd out/The term of your indentures"*
   Luke tempts two young apprentices to cheat their master, his brother.
II.ii. Anne: "I require first/And that since 'tis in fashion"*
   The eligible young Anne sets out her demands for her prospective husband.
II.ii. Mary: "In some part/My sister hath spoke well for the city pleasures"*
   Anne's sister, Mary, demands that she have absolute control over her prospective husband.

III.iii. Luke: "'Twas no fantastic object, but a truth"
> *Given the key and control of his brother's household, Luke revels in his new wealth.*

IV.iv. Luke: "Do not frown;/If you do, I laugh"*
> *Luke accuses his sister-in-law, Lady Frugal, of needless extravagance and announces that he is cutting off her allowance and her servants.*

2 Tragedies

Tragedy and comedy have ancient roots in Greece and Rome. Shakespeare and his contemporaries studied some of the classical plays in school, usually as a means of learning Latin rather than considering their literary or theatrical value. Nonetheless, the Renaissance plays do recall their classical counterparts. According to classical theory, the plot of a tragedy should begin happily but end with death or destruction. Tragic characters should be more important than the everyday person, either royalty, gods, heroes, or generals, so that the fall of the civic leader would be tragic for his or her entire society. This elevated status should be supported with solemn, dignified language and spectacle, and altogether the tragedy should inspire pity and fear in the audience.

Shakespeare and his contemporaries deviated from this model in many interesting ways. For instance, domestic tragedies, such as *A Woman Killed with Kindness,* explore the tragic potential of ordinary citizens. Decadent works, such as *The Revenger's Tragedy,* explore the horrifying potential of sick laughter as well as more dignified grief. Sexual taboos are explored and inverted in the complex tragedies of John Ford and John Webster. And plays such as *Julius Caesar* and

Coriolanus examine the relevance of classical politics for life in seventeenth-century England.

Actors should be familiar with the different types and styles of dramas in order to read and enact them effectively. But the great tragedies of Shakespeare and his contemporaries are necessarily unique and specific in their dramatic effects; the power of *King Lear* or the passion of *Othello* is not easily explained or categorized.

Revenge Tragedies

Revenge tragedy was one of the most popular styles of the early modern stage. It still appeals to audiences in our own age, for instance in cowboy westerns or gang films in which the maverick takes the law into his own hands. This popular form of tragedy had its rebirth with the Renaissance of classical learning. Revenge was a major theme in Greek tragedy (as in Aeschylus' *Oresteia*), but the Elizabethan dramatists were more directly influenced by the Latin tragedies of Seneca. Although most scholars now believe that Seneca wrote his gory dramas to be read, not to be seen onstage, the English dramatists eagerly imported Seneca's ghosts, curses, and horrifying deaths into their theaters.

The revenge tragedy formula begins with a crime, usually a murder, which for some reason goes unpunished. The crime may be skillfully hidden, or the victim may be declared unworthy, or, most often, the society and its leader may be corrupt. When the law fails to serve justice, an individual loyal to the victim is obliged to uncover and avenge the deed. In many of these plays, ghosts encourage the living to exact their revenge: *Hamlet* is the most famous example, but ghosts appear in *The Spanish Tragedy* and *The Atheist's Tragedy*, among others. By taking on the mission of revenge, the revenger steps outside the law of God as well as the law of the state. From this point, the revenger is doomed.

Much of the action in revenge tragedies consists of scheming. The heroes plot to uncover the truth or to test the alleged murderer, while the villains arrange counterplots to cover their tracks. More planning is needed to stage the elaborate revenges, which are often ludicrously theatrical, taking place in the middle of dances (as in *The*

Revenger's Tragedy) or in peculiarly sadistic or suggestive situations. The schemes usually go awry and claim various victims before the intended target is reached. Finally, the avenger himself falls victim to the cycle of retribution.

As the genre evolved, the English revenge tragedies became more and more macabre, with lurid crimes and grotesque acts of retribution. The outrageousness of some of the scenes may indeed provoke what one critic has called "horrid laughter," but beneath the baroque patterns lies a deep uncertainty about where order and righteousness reside in a rapidly changing world. These existential questions are expressed most eloquently in Shakespeare's *Hamlet*, perhaps the greatest of all the English revenge plays.

Shakespeare
Titus Andronicus (c. 1592)

Shakespeare's first tragedy was certainly *Titus Andronicus*. Like almost everything written early in his career, its date of composition is uncertain, but it was written no later than 1592 and perhaps much earlier. *Titus Andronicus* follows the revenge model of Seneca, and employs pseudo-classical characters.

As he did with his classically based comedy, *The Comedy of Errors*, Shakespeare doubles the usual pattern in *Titus Andronicus*. This play is a double revenge drama, and as such, it is doubly violent. The first scene contains two killings: the off-stage ritual sacrifice of the eldest son of Queen Tamora of the Goths, and the on-stage slaying of his own youngest son by Titus. For revenge, Tamora plots the death of Titus' son-in-law, and her surviving sons kidnap, rape, and mutilate his daughter Lavinia. They frame two more of Titus' sons for the murder. In the belief that it will save his condemned sons, Titus is tricked into cutting off his own hand (on-stage), but in vain.

For his own revenge, Titus eventually finds and kills Tamora's sons and bakes them into meat pies served to their mother. In an orgy of death at the play's end, Titus kills Tamora, Titus is killed by the emperor, and the emperor falls to yet another of Titus' sons, all in the space of only three lines.

Until recently, this play has been thought too sensationalistic and crude to be regularly performed, but since World War II it has found new popularity. Deborah Warner's 1987 production for the Royal Shakespeare Company found the combination of intensity and sardonic humor that proved the play to be not only sound, but also highly successful. It still requires great artistry or it turns into a pastiche of Shakespeare, but in the right hands, it is hauntingly powerful.

MONOLOGUE SUGGESTIONS

II.i.1–25. Aaron: "Now climbeth Tamora Olympus' top."
> *The gleeful villain Aaron bawdily brags that he will join Tamora in crime.*

II.iii.10–29. Tamora: "My lovely Aaron, wherefore look'st thou sad"
> *The queen charms her lover, Aaron.*

III.i.1–47. Titus: "Hear me, grave fathers; noble Tribunes stay."
> *Titus begs in vain for the lives of his falsely convicted sons.*

V.i.91–150. Aaron: "'Twas Tamora's two sons that murder'd Bassianus"*
> *Aaron positively crows about the crimes he has committed.*

INTIMATE SCENE SUGGESTIONS

II.iii. *Queen Tamora and her Machiavellian lover, Aaron, plan the rape of Titus' daughter, Lavinia, and Lavinia's husband's death.*

V.ii. *Tamora, trying to pass herself off as the infernal spirit of Revenge, seeks to convince Titus to do her bidding.*

Thomas Kyd (1558–1594)

Among the first wave of the Elizabethan playwrights, Kyd was born six years before Shakespeare and died at the young age of thirty-six. Though he is thought to have written prolifically, only one original play, *The Spanish Tragedy*, has survived. Scholars have been unable to pin down an exact composition date, but it is certainly among the first revenge tragedies and influenced many of the tragedies considered here. *The Spanish Tragedy* was one of the most published and produced plays of the period. Some critics have speculated that Kyd wrote another influential tragedy, called *Hamlet*, now lost, that may have been the immediate source for Shakespeare's play.

Kyd was born to middle-class parents in London and attended the Merchant Taylors' School, which regularly presented theatrical productions. Kyd seems not to have attended university, but he was certainly writing plays for the Queen's company by his mid-twenties. We know little else about him until 1593, when he was detained (and probably tortured) by the Privy Council, which was seeking information about "libelous" writings found in his possession. Kyd swore at the time that the offending writings were those of the late Christopher Marlowe (see later discussion), with whom he had shared a room. He was eventually released but died less than a year later, his death probably precipitated by his treatment while in prison.

The Spanish Tragedy is a gold mine of acting material and contains many levels of theatricality. A ghost and the character of Revenge watch as the intricate plot unfolds. Against the corruption of the Spanish court, old Hieronimo seeks to discover his son's murderers and avenge his death, but grief, madness, and intrigue complicate the relationship between justice and revenge.

The Spanish Tragedy (c. 1582–1587)
MONOLOGUE SUGGESTIONS
II.v. Hieronimo: "What outcries pluck me from my naked bed"
   The father discovers his murdered son.
III.ii. Hieronimo: "What's here? a letter? tush, it is not so!"
   Hieronimo discovers a letter accusing his son's murderers.
III.v. Page: "My master hath forbidden me to look in this box"
   The Page discovers a cruel practical joke.
III.xi. Hieronimo: "There is a path upon your left-hand side"
   Hieronimo declares the damnation of his son's killers.
III.viii. Isabella: "So that, you say, this herb will purge the eye"*
   The grieving mother "runs lunatic" for her lost son.
IV.i. Bel-Imperia: "Is this the love thou bear'st Horatio?"
   She urges Hieronimo to avenge Horatio's death.
IV.ii. Isabella: "Tell me no more! O monstrous homicides!"
   Isabella curses the place of her son's murder and kills herself.

Cyril Tourneur (c. 1580–1626)
Tourneur's biography, like those of so many Elizabethan dramatists, remains extremely vague. However, Tourneur clearly had a fascinating career as a civil servant, serving Sir Francis Vere, possibly during the Dutch wars, and Sir Edward Cecil, with whom he sailed to Cadiz in 1625, a voyage that led to Tourneur's death in Ireland in 1626.

Between these prestigious appointments, Tourneur seems to have spent about a decade as a professional writer in London, where he published several plays and funeral poems and contributed to at least one collaborative script. Tourneur is the undisputed author of The Atheist's Tragedy and the author traditionally credited with The Revenger's Trag-

edy, the influential work that established the satirical, decadent tone associated with Jacobean revenge tragedy. However, many twentieth-century scholars have attributed the play to Middleton. Regardless of its author or authors, *The Revenger's Tragedy* is an exciting, gruesome play in which Vindice carries out a series of grotesque revenges against the debauched Italian court. *The Atheist's Tragedy* takes the idea of the revenger, who acts outside God's law as well as the state's, to a metaphysical extreme; the atheist D'Amville is a nihilist whose vengeful crimes finally lead him to destroy himself.

The Revenger's Tragedy (1606) (Also see Middleton)
MONOLOGUE SUGGESTIONS

I.i. Vindice: "Duke! Royal lecher! Go, grey hair'd adultery!"
Holding the skull of his murdered lover, Vindice plots against the members of the guilty court.

I.ii. Duchess: "Was't ever known step-duchess was so mild"
The Duchess plans to take revenge on her husband by cuckolding him with his bastard son.

I.ii. Spurio: "Duke, thou didst do me wrong, and by thy act"
The bastard declares that adultery comes naturally to him.

II.i. Vindice: "O, think upon the pleasure of the palace!"*
The disguised Vindice tempts his mother with the luxury available at the court.

SCENE SUGGESTIONS

I.iii. *Lussurioso hires the disguised Vindice as a pander to procure Castiza, Vindice's sister.*

II.i. *The disguised Vindice persuades his mother to send her daughter Castiza to Lussurioso.*

IV.iv. *Castiza tests her mother Gratiana's virtue.*

The Atheist's Tragedy (1611)
MONOLOGUE SUGGESTIONS

I.iv. Levidulcia: "Nature, the loving mother of us all"*
The bawdy Levidulcia urges her daughter Castabella to enjoy the pleasures of the flesh now rather than wait for her absent lover.

II.i. Borachio: "The enemy, defeated of a fair"
The disguised Borachio improvises an exciting description of a recent battle.

II.vi. Charlemont: "O my affrighted soul! what fearful dream"
Charlemont awakes after his murdered father's ghost appeared to him in a dream.
IV.iii. Castabella: "Now Heav'n defend me! May my memory"*
Castabella recoils against her uncle D'Amville's attempted rape.
IV.iii. D'Amville: "Why dost thou stare upon me? Thou art not"
The sight of a skull makes D'Amville recollect his crimes.

SCENE SUGGESTIONS
II.iv. *The atheist D'Amville and his henchman Borachio celebrate the success of their plot to murder Montferrers, D'Amville's brother.*
III.i. *The lovers Castabella and Charlemont are reunited in secrecy at Charlemont's father's grave.*

Francis Beaumont (c. 1584–1616) and
John Fletcher (1579–1625)
As well as writing various plays independently and with other partners, Beaumont and Fletcher collaborated on a series of very popular plays for the Jacobean theater. They were most famous for tragicomedies, and some selections from these works, along with some biographical information, appear in Chapter 4 of this book.

Their revenge tragedy, *The Maid's Tragedy*, is one of the more sensitive works of the genre. Within the corrupt court setting, popular in many of the Jacobean revenge tragedies, Beaumont and Fletcher give priority to the emotional experiences of the characters, rather than the theatrics of crime and revenge. The plot involves a young hero, Amintor, who is taken from his beloved Aspatia to become the token husband of the king's corrupted mistress, Evadne. The revenge is instigated by Evadne's brother Melantius, also Amintor's friend, who claims his sister's dishonor as his own. *The Maid's Tragedy* contains beautiful examples of Beaumont and Fletcher's lyric verse; Aspatia's speeches of despair are particularly haunting.

The Maid's Tragedy (c. 1611)
MONOLOGUE SUGGESTIONS
II.ii. Aspatia: "Alas, poor wenches!"*
After seeing her betrothed Amintor married to Evadne at the king's command, Aspatia weeps for disappointed women.

III.i. Amintor: "You that can know to wrong, should know how men"*
> *Amintor draws his sword to avenge his honor as a husband but is confounded by his reverence for the king.*

V.ii. Evadne: "The night grows horrible, and all about me"
> *Evadne enters the king's bedchamber and prepares to kill him.*

SCENE SUGGESTIONS

II.i. *Evadne explains to her new husband Amintor that she will never consummate their marriage because she is the king's mistress.*

III.ii. *Amintor confides to his friend and brother-in-law Melantius that Evadne is exploited as the king's lover.*

IV.i. *Melantius confronts his sister Evadne and persuades her to help him kill the king.*

V.ii. *Evadne wakes and confronts the king before stabbing him.*

George Chapman (c. 1560–1634)

Although Chapman had considerable success in the theater with a wide range of plays, he is remembered primarily for his English translations of the works of Homer, which he called "the Worke that I was borne to doe." Chapman's early biography is typically vague; although he seems to have attended Oxford, and possibly Cambridge, and had a passing connection with the Inner Temple, Chapman never received a degree and appears to be largely self-educated. Like his colleague Ben Jonson (with whom he collaborated on *Eastward Ho!*), Chapman had a formidable command of classical learning and philosophy, and many of his plays express Stoicism in the figures of "Senecal men." Chapman translated the *Iliad* (1611) and the *Odyssey* (1615) into English for the first time, and championed these important works for the rest of his life. However, like many of his ambitious colleagues, Chapman found that he could not support himself with poetry alone and turned to the theater to make a living.

Chapman's tragedy, *Bussy D'Ambois* (c. 1604), was based on recent French history. In that play, Chapman presents the historical title character as a malcontented philosopher who rises through the courts of Monsieur (the historical Alençon) and King Henry III, only to seduce Tamyra, the wife of the Count Montsurry, who murders Bussy and tortures Tamyra. Several years later, Chapman wrote an entirely nonhistorical sequel, *The Revenge of Bussy D'Ambois* (c. 1611), in which Bussy's invented brother, Clermont d'Ambois, seeks revenge against Montsurry, only to find that the King is also treacherous and Machiavellian. Clermont is essentially a Stoic philosopher who insists that happiness and integrity can only be found within, not in the emotional claims of love or melodramatic revenge. One of the main interests of the play is to see this principled hero struggle to act within the cynical, highly emotive world typical of revenge tragedy.

The Revenge of Bussy D'Ambois (c. 1611)
MONOLOGUE SUGGESTIONS
I.i. Clermont: "Nay, we must now have nothing brought on stages"*
   Clermont defends the stage as a way for people to learn to bear the ups and downs of life.
I.ii. Tamyra: "Revenge, that ever red sitt'st in the eyes"
   Tamyra calls the spirit of revenge to avenge her dead lover, Bussy D'Ambois.
II.i. Clermont: "They are the breathing sepulchres of noblesse"
   Hearing that Montsurry would not accept his challenge, Clermont curses the loss of true nobility and honor in France.
IV.i. Aumale: "What spirit breathes thus in this more than man"
   Captain Aumale describes Clermont's passion in battle like a force of nature.
IV.iii. Countess of Cambrai: "What change is here? How are my hopes prevented?"
   Learning of the King's ambush of Clermont, the Countess rails against his treachery.
V.i. Clermont: "In love of women, my affection first"*
   Clermont prefers the spiritual love of friendship to the sensual, transitory love of women.
V.v. Clermont: "Shall I live, and he"*
   Despairing that he may not honorably take revenge against the treacherous King, Clermont decides to take his own life.

SCENE SUGGESTION
III.ii. *When Clermont refuses to act after receiving an anonymous letter, his sister Charlotte accuses him and his comrade Renel of cowardice.*

Major Tragedies

Shakespeare
Though Shakespeare experimented widely in different genres, he is best known for his major tragedies. Many a person who has never heard of *The Winter's Tale* or *Two Gentlemen of Verona* could instantly identify *Romeo and Juliet* and *Hamlet* as Shakespeare plays.

For the actor, the public's familiarity with these works is both a blessing and a curse. An audience with some background will come enthusiastically into the theater, and may know the general plot of the play well enough to allow the actors to place their attention on characterization rather than exposition. On the other hand, people who know little about the canon may still have very strong opinions about how Lear or Macbeth should be played. They may be surprisingly familiar with particular interpretations of Hamlet's role, through such films as Kenneth Branagh's, for example. Undertaking the major tragic roles often means placing oneself in direct comparison with some of the great artists of our time.

For these reasons, the following monologue and scene lists may tend toward the quirky and off-beat selections rather than the most familiar. A monologue pieced together from a *Hamlet* scene, for example, may have far greater impact in an audition than one of the well-known soliloquies, because it is both familiar and fresh. Scene work featuring lesser-known characters from great plays can be more rewarding than living directly in Laurence Olivier's shadow, especially for the novice.

Romeo and Juliet (c. 1594)
Shakespeare's retelling of the tale of the doomed love of Romeo and Juliet is so familiar that it needs little introduction. It is perhaps his most popular play.

This play shares several features with the mature comedies. It seems for most of the first three acts to be following the conventions of the romantic comedies rather than heading for full-blown tragedy. Particularly in the characters of the Nurse and Mercutio we find the ridiculing of romance we associate with comedies. Another important feature is the sheer poetic intensity of the piece. Not only in the "balcony" scene, but in almost all of the lovers' interchanges we find highly rhetorical and theatrical dialogue.

These qualities make the play superb material for young actors, even if it is familiar. The challenge of the material is great, but the benefits of mastering it are immense.

SHARED SONNET SUGGESTION
I.v.92–109. "If I profane with my unworthiest hand"
Romeo and Juliet share this sonnet at their first meeting.

MONOLOGUE SUGGESTIONS
III.iii.17–51. Romeo: "There is no world without Verona walls"
The banished Romeo wails out his misery and distress.
III.ii.1–31. Juliet: "Gallop apace, you fiery-footed steeds"
Juliet cannot wait for her new husband to join her for their wedding night.
V.i.1–16, 34–57. Romeo: "If I may trust the flattering truth of sleep" plus "Well, Juliet, I will lie with thee tonight"
Romeo decides to die to be with his Juliet.

INTIMATE SCENE SUGGESTIONS
II.ii. *The balcony scene.*
II.iii. *The Friar counsels Romeo to slow down but agrees finally to marry him to Juliet.*
II.v. *The Nurse teases Juliet by withholding information about the outcome of the previous scene.*
III.ii. *Hearing of Tybalt's death at Romeo's hands, Juliet refuses to condemn him and convinces the Nurse to bring him to spend their wedding night.*
III.iii. *The Friar helps the distraught Romeo collect himself and consider his banishment more calmly.*
IV.i. *The Friar conceives of a desperate plan to help Juliet with a "magic" potion.*

PUBLIC SCENE SUGGESTIONS
I.iv. *Romeo and his friend, Mercutio, taunt each other while on the way with their friends to "crash" the Capulet ball.*
II.iv. *Juliet's Nurse meets Romeo (who is with his rowdy friends) to convey a message to him from her mistress.*

Hamlet (c. 1601)
When we think of Shakespeare, it is *Hamlet* that first and foremost springs to mind. On the simplest level, this play is a revenge trag-

edy, which, in his inimitable way, Shakespeare twists into a double revenge tragedy with Laertes' return late in the play. Because of its philosophical depth and metaphysical mystery, however, *Hamlet* has become much more than we expect of revenge plays. Where they are often crude, this play is the epitome of sophistication. Where they are driven by passions for revenge, this one has a frustrating restraint at its center. Hamlet delays his revenge far beyond what could be expected of any reasonable man, for reasons that have kept critics speculating for centuries.

Hamlet was composed in Shakespeare's mid-career, after a period in which he had been preoccupied with comedies and histories. It dates well after *Romeo and Juliet*. In it Shakespeare brings new depth to the tragic form, perhaps arising from life experience that now included the death of his father, a beloved brother, and his only son.

There are no easy routes into *Hamlet*. It is the most admired, most analyzed, most imitated play in history. Everyone has an opinion and a pet approach. Dealing with it is a matter of rolling up one's sleeves and being ready for the inevitable combination of flack and praise that comes with fresh approaches.

In auditions and scene study, a humble approach is recommended. The material is rich and rewarding but is subject to more scrutiny than any other choice that could be made. Approach the great soliloquies with particular caution.

MONOLOGUE SUGGESTIONS

Hamlet has several famous soliloquies: at I.ii.129–159; II.ii.526–582; III.i.58–92; III.iii.358–369; and IV.iv.20–56—but the following suggestions are for speeches from other characters or are pieced together from Hamlet's scenes of dialogue to avoid the use of overexposed material.

I.ii.196–212. Horatio: "Two nights together had these gentlemen"
   Hamlet's best friend explains how he came to encounter the ghost of Hamlet's father.
I.iii.1–44. Laertes: "My necessaries are inbarqued. Farewell."*
   As he leaves on a voyage, Laertes warns his sister against involvement with Hamlet.
I.iii.55–81. Polonius: "Yet here, Laertes? Aboard, aboard, for shame!"

Laertes' father has plenty of free advice for his son as he leaves for foreign travel.

I.iv.9–18.22. Hamlet: "The King doth wake tonight and take his rouse"*

In a textually complex passage, Hamlet surveys the corruption all around him.

I.v.9–91. Ghost: "I am thy father's spirit"*

In a long speech, the ghost of Hamlet's father reveals his murder and demands revenge.

III.i.149–160. Ophelia: "O what a noble mind is here o'erthrown"

Ophelia's shocked reaction to Hamlet's cruelty toward her.

III.iii.36–72. Claudius: "O, my offense is rank! It smells to heaven."

The corrupt king tries, and fails, to pray.

III.iv.52–78. Hamlet: "Look here upon this picture, and on this"

Distraught, Hamlet confronts his mother over her remarriage.

IV.vii.134–154. Gertrude: "One woe doth tread upon another's heel"

The Queen has to tell Laertes his sister has drowned.

V.ii.1–81. Hamlet: "So much for this, sir. Now, let me see, the other"*

Hamlet tells Horatio how he escaped Claudius' plot against his life.

INTIMATE SCENE SUGGESTIONS

I.ii. *Hamlet's friend, Horatio, tells him of the appearance of the ghost.*

I.v. *Hamlet encounters his father's ghost, who tells Hamlet of his murder.*

II.i. *Ophelia reports to her father of Hamlet's wild appearance in her chamber.*

III.i. *Hamlet visits his mother's room to confront her about her part in the murder of his father. Hamlet kills the hiding Polonius, and again sees the ghost.*

III.i. *Ophelia tries to break off her relationship with Hamlet but is surprised by the intensity of his reaction.*

V.i. *Two grave diggers make light of death while working on Ophelia's grave.*

V.i. *Hamlet trades quips with a gravedigger, unaware of whose grave they joke over.*

PUBLIC SCENE SUGGESTIONS

I.ii.64–128. *In front of the whole court, Hamlet sets out to shame his mother, Gertrude, and her new husband, Claudius, for their failure to grieve as deeply as he does.*

IV.iii. *In front of courtiers, Hamlet taunts Claudius about the whereabouts of the corpse of Polonius.*

Othello (c. 1603)

The tragedy of the Moor of Venice is a remarkable piece, which surprisingly evades many of the problems inherent in Shakespeare's earlier play set in the same city, *The Merchant of Venice*. Where Shylock is a more humanized but still recognizable stage "Jew," Othello is a complete reversal of the conventional stage "Moor," usually a ruthless, uncivilized buffoon. Shakespeare had written stereotyped Moorish characters in his earlier years. The Machiavellian Aaron in *Titus* is one, and in comic proportions, so is Morocco in *The Merchant of Venice*. Othello, however, reverses the type. He is a noble soldier, while Othello's right-hand man, Iago, is the Machiavellian villain. Shakespeare clearly intended to reverse the stereotypes. Although the play contains many racist epithets, they are not implicitly condoned as in *The Merchant of Venice*. Here our sympathies lie with the misled Othello. We can see and condemn the racism to which he is subjected.

The plot of the play is domestic rather than national or cosmic in scope and deals with human interaction at the personal level. Iago dupes Othello into believing that his wife Desdemona has betrayed him by taking Cassio as a lover. Acting on this belief, Othello takes his wife's life. His error is exposed and he takes his own life. In the process, Iago's wife Emilia is killed, but not before she unravels the whole plot. Iago is headed for certain death when the curtain falls.

MONOLOGUE SUGGESTIONS

I.iii.127–168. Othello: "Her father loved me, oft invited me"
   The Moorish hero tells exactly how he wooed and won his bride.
I.iii.247–258. Desdemona: "That I did love the Moor to live with him"
   Desdemona pleads to go with her husband to war rather than stay behind where she is not wanted.
II.iii.310–336. Iago: "And what's he then that says I play the villain"
   In soliloquy, Iago delights that he can use others' goodness against them.
V.i.84–101. Emilia: "But I do think it is their husbands' faults"
   Desdemona's servant offers a surprisingly modern, proto-feminist viewpoint on infidelity.
V.ii.1–22. Othello: "It is the cause, it is the cause, my soul."
   The agonized soliloquy in which Othello decides he must kill his wife.

V.ii.347–369. Othello: "Soft you; a word or two before you go."*
Othello's death speech.

INTIMATE SCENE SUGGESTIONS

I.iii. *Iago persuades the despairing Roderigo that he still may have a chance for love with Othello's new bride, Desdemona.*

II.iii. *Iago seduces Cassio into asking Desdemona to plead for his reputation.*

III.iii. *Iago fuels Othello's suspicions about his wife's fidelity.*

III.iii. *Desdemona, as she was asked, pleads for Cassio to her husband.*

III.iv. *Emilia, a lady-in-waiting, calms Desdemona about her husband's jealousy.*

III.iv. *Othello asks his wife for her handkerchief, believing (wrongly) that she has given it to Cassio as a love token.*

IV.ii. *Roderigo confronts Iago about his lies but is filled again with false hope.*

V.ii. *Pushed over the emotional brink, Othello kills his wife.*

Macbeth (c. 1606)

Macbeth dates from 1606, several years into the reign of James I, but was not published until the First Folio of 1623. This text, the only edition we have, shows signs of being a shortened version of a longer, lost original and includes material interpolated from another play, Middleton's *The Witch.* We don't know when or why the changes were made, or most especially, by whom. The text, therefore, presents some unresolvable difficulties.

The play, as we now have it, is a fast-moving one, filled with visceral excitement. The supernatural element presented by the three witches (and occasionally by their leader, Hecate, though she is often cut) lends a mystical air. Numerous battle scenes and scenes of escalating violence give it motion, while a "mad" scene for Macbeth's sleepwalking wife and the appearance of a ghost give it spiritual power.

The protagonist of the play comes to the throne of Scotland through intrigue and murder. Like *Richard III,* the play mostly concerns the central character's attempt to hold onto the throne as his crimes exact an increasingly personal toll. Macbeth, however, has a far more active conscience and suffers more for his actions than does Richard. He is eventually hunted down and driven from power by a coalition of "good" characters, including Malcolm, the rightful heir, and Macduff, the avenging soldier.

The extractable material from this play is exciting and complex. The characters often undertake actions about which they are deeply ambivalent, allowing actors to show range and depth. The challenge is to show the steps toward a decision, and the slow dawning of all the consequences after the action has been taken.

MONOLOGUE SUGGESTIONS

I.ii.7–42. Captain: "Doubtful it stood"*
  A bleeding sergeant relates the events of the day's battle.
I.v.1–28, 36–52. Lady Macbeth: "They met me in the day of success"
  Upon receipt of a letter telling of the witches' prophecy of kingship, Lady Macbeth begins to think about what it will take to move her husband to success, and takes action.
I.vii.1–28. Macbeth: "If it were done when 'tis done, then 'twere well"
  The thane thinks through the consequences of his assassination plan and balks at it.
II.i.33–64. Macbeth: "Is this a dagger I see before me"
  Macbeth proceeds toward the murder, despite misgivings and even hallucinations.
II.iii.1–20. Porter: "Here's a knocking indeed!"
  The porter pretends that he is the keeper of Hell's gate.
III.1.49–73. Macbeth: "To be thus is nothing"
  Macbeth becomes more obsessed with the prophecy that Banquo will father a line of kings.
III.v.2–34. Hecate: "Have I not reason, beldams as you are?"
  In rhyming lines, the witches' leader plans the next moves against Macbeth.

INTIMATE SCENE SUGGESTIONS

I.vii. *When Macbeth is ready to back out of the plot to kill the king, his wife shames him into going forward.*
II.ii. *Macbeth murders the king but is shattered by the action, so his wife has to clean up both the literal and metaphorical mess.*
IV.iii. *Macduff comes to urge the rightful heir to take up the battle against Macbeth, but Malcolm is cautious. First, Macduff must pass his tests.*

King Lear (c. 1605)
King Lear is not Shakespeare's most popular work, but critically it is often accounted as the greatest. Shakespeare takes an old folktale

and creates from it something akin to a religious ritual. The tragedy unfolds from an unwise king who would divide his country into three parts by asking which of his three daughters loves him best, but then judges their responses incorrectly. The king's wise fool, who teaches through fooling, is another folk element. However, no "folk-lore" tone intrudes into this dazzlingly elevated work. *King Lear* is set in pre-Christian Britain and is filled with religious invocations and imagery. The suffering of the king, his loyal followers, and his loving daughter Cordelia is constant and almost ritualized.

Part of the impression of ritual derives from the Gloucester sub-plot, which is a perfect mirror of the main plot. In it, Gloucester incorrectly trusts his bastard son, Edmund, and rejects his legitimate one, Edgar. The two plots echo and reinforce each other. The repetition creates a fatalistic sense—if not of the preordained, then at least of the inevitability of the outcome.

Lear and Gloucester are, of course, unlikely roles for young or inexperienced actors. Their offspring, however, are all superb roles with excellent extractable materials.

MONOLOGUE SUGGESTIONS

I.ii.1–22. Edmund: "Thou, nature, art my goddess. To thy law"
Edmund decries his illegitimacy.

I.ii.108–121. Edmund: "This is the excellent foppery of the world"
Astrology aside, Edmund knows that he would be what he is under any conditions.

I.iv.166–179. Goneril: "Not only, sir, this your all-licensed fool"
Lear's daughter blasts her father for the behavior of his retinue.

II.iii.158–178. Edgar: "I heard myself proclaimed"
Unjustly accused of a murder plot, Edgar plans his strategy for escape.

III.ii.1–24. Lear: "Blow, winds, and crack your cheeks! rage! Blow!"
For those up for the biggest challenge, this is a speech that rivals the powers of nature.

IV.vii.14–42. Cordelia: "O you kind gods"*
Cordelia finds her father in a state of desperate ill health.

INTIMATE SCENE SUGGESTIONS

I.ii. *The bastard son, Edmund, tricks his gullible father into believing his legitimate son is trying to kill him.*

II.i. *To push his case further, Edmund displays to his father the "wound" Edgar has given him.*
IV.ii. *Albany suspects his wife, Goneril, of treachery. She, in turn, thinks him weak.* *
IV.vi. *Driven into disguise, Edgar leads his blind father, Gloucester, to believe that he has jumped from the cliffs of Dover and survived.*

PUBLIC SCENE SUGGESTION

II.iv.184–281. *Lear confronts his daughter, Regan, and discovers she has no loyalty to him.* *

Christopher Marlowe (1564–1593)

Shakespeare's preeminence as a tragic dramatist is rivaled only by Christopher Marlowe, one of the earliest playwrights represented in this volume. Like Shakespeare, Marlowe brought extraordinary poetic gifts to the stage, along with a biting wit and a keen sense for exciting spectacle. Although all his plays are considered tragedies, Marlowe exploited the possibilities of history and comedy within the tragic form. For instance, his best-known play, *Doctor Faustus*, uses pageantry and farce to lure his audience to the brink of damnation and despair. Marlowe's ambitious theatricality cleared the way for his successors to imagine new possibilities for the classical tragic form.

The life and death of Christopher Marlowe are veiled in mystery. He was born in the same year as Shakespeare into a shoemaker's family. In Canterbury he attended the King's School, which regularly produced plays. He earned a bachelor of arts degree from Cambridge University when he was twenty, but his master's degree was nearly withheld by University authorities because of excessive absences. High government officials mysteriously intervened, saying that Marlowe had been engaged "in matters touching the benefit of his country," presumably international espionage. During his life in London, from 1587–1593, Marlowe was caught in numerous scandals for atheism, brawling, and homosexuality, yet he also produced numerous poems and seven plays that radically reshaped the English drama. In May of 1593, Marlowe was awaiting trial for heresy before the Privy Council when he was killed in a tavern brawl in Deptford. The mysteries about Marlowe's killers (who were also government agents), the quick inquest, and its hasty cover-up have never been explained.

While at Cambridge, Marlowe translated Latin poems by Ovid and Lucan into English verse, and his first play, *Dido, Queen of Carthage*, written with Thomas Nashe, was also based on classical sources. The two parts of *Tamburlaine the Great*, played by Edward Alleyn with the Lord Admiral's Men, established Marlowe's fame on the London stage. This tale of an extraordinary shepherd who rose to conquer the world caught the imagination of the audience in a time of unparalleled social upheaval and individualism. Tamburlaine is the first in a series of Marlovian anti-heroes (all played by Alleyn) known as "over-reachers," exceptional individuals driven by ambition to exceed all limitations, only to fall like Icarus from an astonishing height. (Shakespeare's *Coriolanus* and *Macbeth* adapt this tragic formula.) Amidst a wealth of pageantry and comic by-play, *Doctor Faustus* recounts the dark legend of a scholar who contracts with the devil for knowledge and power. The Machiavellian Barabas in *The Jew of Malta* schemes for profit in ever more outrageous schemes until he is finally caught and boiled in oil (on stage). In both of these plays, Marlowe manipulates medieval stereotypes to achieve what T. S. Eliot termed a kind of farce, "a terribly serious, even savage humor." *The Massacre at Paris* dramatizes the bloody 1572 attempt by the Duke of Guise and his Catholic followers to slaughter the Huguenots in France. In *Edward II*, Marlowe, like Shakespeare, turns to Holinshed's Chronicles for source material from English history. This complex play traces the shifting alliances between the King, his favorite Gaveston, the Queen, and the rebellious barons, led by Mortimer. (Selections from *Edward II* appear in chapter 3 of this book.)

All seven plays are characterized by extraordinary poetry, informed by Marlowe's classical education. Marlowe disdained "the jigging veins of rhyming mother wits" and replaced his predecessors' doggerel with a confident, heavy iambic pentameter that his admiring contemporary Ben Jonson called "Marlowe's mighty line." Marlowe's verse drives his characters' ambitions; the long speeches climb from one action to the next. The frequent allusions to exotic places and classical names reflect the characters' glamorous fantasies of godlike power. Marlowe's characters often use hyperbole, a figure of speech that exceeds realistic limitations, such as "the topless towers" or "fairer than whitest snow." Actors who can use this heady language to advance their characters' audacious objectives will find that Marlowe invites them to act in a world that is larger than life. Let the verse form help you find the magnificent self-assuredness of Marlowe's characters.

Tamburlaine the Great (Part 1, c. 1587; Part 2, c. 1588)
MONOLOGUE SUGGESTIONS

Part 1, II.iii. Tamburlaine: "And so, mistake you not a whit, my lord"
   Tamburlaine predicts the glories of war.
Part 1, V.i. Zenocrate: "Wretched Zenocrate, that liv'st to see"*
   Tamburlaine's wife mourns the horrors of the wars.
Part 2, III.ii. Tamburlaine: "But now my boys, leave off, and list to me"
   Tamburlaine instructs his sons in the arts of war.
Part 2, III.ii. Tamburlaine: "Villain, art thou the son of Tamburlaine"
   Tamburlaine scorns his son's fear and displays his own courage.

Doctor Faustus (c. 1588–1593)
MONOLOGUE SUGGESTION

V.ii. Faustus: "Ah, Faustus/Now hast thou but one bare hour to live"
   Faustus finally recognizes his damnation and prays for mercy.

INTIMATE SCENE SUGGESTIONS

I.iii. *Faustus conjures Mephostophilis, who appears dressed as a friar.*
II.i. *Despite sudden doubts, Faustus seals his contract with Mephostophilis.*

The Jew of Malta (c. 1589)
INTIMATE SCENE SUGGESTIONS

I.ii. *Barabas and his daughter Abigall plot to disguise her as a nun.*
III.iv. *Barabas and his servant Ithimore plot to poison a nunnery.*

Tragedies of Classical Times

Tragedy is, of course, a classical form rehabilitated in the Renaissance. Fifteenth- and early sixteenth-century writers began by translating the Greek and Roman works, then adapting them, and then imitating them in original plays. Schoolboys studied and performed these works along with the rest of their classical studies, which ensured that they were familiar with the history of Greece and Rome. The exciting classical stories of political intrigue, assassination, and war were at the fingertips of Shakespeare and his contemporaries when they looked for new dramatic material. Many dramatists seem to have begun their careers with classically styled work, among them, Marlowe's *Dido, Queen of Carthage*, Shakespeare's *Titus Andronicus*, and Chapman's *Caesar and Pompey*.

The classical tragedies of the early modern stage often explore provocative political themes under the guise of history. Actors can explore the showmanship of classical rhetoric within some of the exciting speeches of these plays.

Shakespeare
Julius Caesar (c. 1600)

Because it can be used to teach lessons about history and government, and because it contains no sex, this is the play that everyone reads in school. It is probably the most despised play in the canon. In many ways, the play deserves neither the reputation that caused schools to choose it in the first place, nor the one that reluctant students have given it. It is neither so instructive nor so preachy as most think. The play presents a finely balanced moral dilemma—whether the fear of what a leader might do is cause enough to remove him—but does not provide any neat solutions.

Like so many of the histories, this play is named for the ruler at the time of the events, not its central character. The tragedy is really Brutus'. He is seduced into joining a conspiracy on the basis of attractive arguments, none of which are really justification for the action they endorse. He is the tragic hero who falls from a high moral state into decline and death.

Brutus begins having doubts immediately after the murder, and his attempt to control Caesar's funeral ceremony makes one wonder if he is any less inclined to the dictatorship than the man he helped assassinate. Brutus' coolly rational approach to the Roman people is no match for Antony's emotional rhetoric, however, and he is thrown into a civil war. His side eventually loses, in no small part due to his quavering doubts.

The Roman subject of the play is matched by its style, an intentionally austere narrative. The almost clinical rhetoric of the speeches provides fine examples of the patterns of classical speechmaking and argumentation. *Julius Caesar* also gives an intriguing insight into Shakespeare's cooler side. The slow seduction of Brutus and his long period of regret can be very useful for actors who are prone to sweeping generalities of emotion to work on subtle increments of meaning.

MONOLOGUE SUGGESTIONS

I.ii.92–162. Cassius: "I know that virtue to be in you, Brutus"*
Cassius reduces the high and mighty Caesar to human proportions for Brutus.

I.ii.199–215. Caesar: "Let me have men about me that are fat"
Caesar expresses misgivings about the noblemen around him.

II.i.10–34. Brutus: "It must be by his death. And for my part"
Brutus rationalizes himself into the assassination plot.

II.i.236–255. Portia: "You've ungently, Brutus"
Brutus' wife attempts to soothe her husband, though she is not sure what causes his nervousness.

II.ii.8–30. Calpurnia: "What mean you Caesar? Think you to walk forth?"
Caesar's wife has had visions of his death and tries, in vain, to keep him home.

III.i.257–278. Antony: "O pardon me, thou bleeding piece of earth"
Antony had to pretend he concurred in Caesar's assassination, but once alone he reveals his true feelings.

III.ii.70–102, 163–191. Antony: "Friends, Romans, Countrymen" and "If you have tears, prepare to shed them now."
In twin speeches, Antony incites the crowds to riots. If you have memorized the first of these before, look especially at the second, which reveals new insights into Antony.

INTIMATE SCENE SUGGESTIONS

I.ii. *The "lean and hungry" Cassius slowly tempts Brutus into conspiracy.*
II.i. *Brutus' wife, Portia, graphically proves that she is strong enough to be trusted with whatever secret Brutus harbors.*
II.ii. *Caesar's wife, Calpurnia, begs him not to go to the senate.*
IV.ii, IV.iii. *In two successive scenes, the friendship of Brutus and Cassius is strained to the breaking point.*

Antony and Cleopatra (c. 1606)
Antony and Cleopatra is, in many ways, *Romeo and Juliet* writ large. The scope of the play is immense, with more scenes than any other

Shakespeare play, covering the entire western world of Roman times, but the drama is essentially the story of two sensually intoxicated lovers whose interaction dooms them.

The play is not a direct sequel to *Julius Caesar*, but it is the same Antony of that play later in his life. (The character named Caesar in this script is Octavius Caesar, nephew of Julius Caesar.) Antony is part of the ruling triumvirate that succeeds Caesar, but both of his co-rulers, Pompey and Octavius, are itching for a larger share of the power, and war breaks out within the empire. While Antony idles with Cleopatra in Egypt, his troops fight a war without him and his power slips away. Under the emotional and political pressures of war, Cleopatra betrays Antony, a move that leads finally to his suicide and then to hers, as she hastens to join him in the afterlife.

When Antony and Cleopatra are together, the voluptuousness of their language is overwhelming. Shakespeare is writing about middle-aged people, but he does so with the sensual directness, even bawdiness, of his youthful plays. The capricious queen, whose vanity is matched only by her capacity for devotion, is one of Shakespeare's richest characters. Even the cynical captain, Enobarbus, sees the charm of Cleopatra. His description of her is one of the most famous and most opulent speeches in Shakespeare.

The poetry of this piece is indulgently beautiful at times. A fascinating quality of the script is the way that comedy is intertwined with seriousness throughout. Especially in scenes in which Cleopatra interacts with messengers (including the one that brings her the asp for her suicide) there is apt to be a strong comic tone.

MONOLOGUE SUGGESTIONS

I.iv.16–33. Octavius Caesar: "You are too indulgent."
Caesar, though in his early twenties, feels free to chide the older, weaker Lepidus.

I.iv.55–71. Octavius Caesar: "Antony/Leave thy lascivious wassails"
To the absent Antony, Caesar aims a plea to return to martial honor.

I.v.18–34. Cleopatra: "O, Charmian"
Erotically, Cleopatra imagines where Antony is.

II.ii.196–211. Enobarbus: "The barge she sat in, like a burnished throne"
The speech of description referenced earlier.

IV.xiii.9–49. Antony: "All is lost."
> *Enraged by the loss of a battle and Cleopatra's treachery, Antony rants against everyone.*

IV.xv.1–22. Antony: "Eros, thou yet behold'st me?"*
> *Antony enters, seeking revenge against Cleopatra, but after a knowing self-examination, ends by deciding to commit suicide.*

IV.xvi.75–93. Cleopatra: "No more but e'en a woman, and commanded"
> *Swooning at the death of Antony, Cleopatra decides how to handle the body.*

V.ii.73–93. Cleopatra: "No matter, sir, what I have seen or known"
> *After Antony's death, Cleopatra memorializes him.*

V.ii.271–289. Cleopatra: "Give me my robe. Put on the crown."
> *Cleopatra prepares for her death.*

INTIMATE SCENE SUGGESTIONS

II.v. *Cleopatra cruelly (comically) mistreats the messenger bringing her news of Antony's remarriage.*

IV.xiv. *Antony plans his suicide with his servant Eros.*

IV.xv. *Antony's death scene in Cleopatra's arms.*

V.ii. *Cleopatra takes delivery of the fatal asp from the comic messenger known only as Clown.*

PUBLIC SCENE SUGGESTIONS

I.i. *In the midst of her court, Cleopatra distracts Antony from messengers from Rome.*

I.iii. *Sending a decidedly mixed message, Cleopatra finally agrees that Antony must return to Rome to attend to business.*

Coriolanus (c. 1608)

Coriolanus is set in the early days of the Roman republic, when Rome was one of several warring cities, not yet the dominant power it would become. The plot takes place within the exceedingly martial culture of an embattled city and an emergent republic. The noble class, called the patricians, have expelled Rome's repressive kings but are not willing to empower the lower class, the plebeians. Many Romans hope the warrior-hero Caius Martius, who is given the title of "Coriolanus" for conquering the city of Corioli, will become consul, but he refuses to bow to the plebeian masses to be "elected." He is a soldier, not a politician, and he will not learn their trade. Coriolanus has obviously received his iron will from his mother, Volumnia, who urges unyielding resistance to compromise throughout most of the play.

When Coriolanus is banished as a danger to the new republic, he chooses to destroy his ungrateful home city, allying himself with his hated enemy, Tullus Aufidius, leader of the Volsci. His attack on Rome is averted only when his mother, wife, and child come to beg him to reconsider. Coriolanus backs down and dies brutally at the hands of the troops he would have led against Rome, but the city is saved.

In tone, this play is an almost exact opposite of *Antony and Cleopatra*. Where that play is relaxed and sensuous, this one is tense and brutal. The martial virtues are instilled so deeply that even mothers hope for their children's involvement in battle. The extractable material has the steely quality of the play throughout, making for high contrast with softer tragedies and comedies.

MONOLOGUE SUGGESTIONS
I.iii.1–21. Volumnia: "I pray you daughter sing"
> *Coriolanus' mother exposes a bloodthirstiness and ambition of enormous proportions.*

III.iii.124–139. Coriolanus: "You common cry of curs, whose breath I hate"
> *Refusing to play politician, Coriolanus cuts all ties to his city rather than flatter the multitude.*

IV.iv.12–26. Coriolanus: "O world, thy slippery turns! Friends now fast sworn"
> *The exiled warrior muses on the reversal of his fortunes.*

IV.v.64–99. Coriolanus: "My name is Caius Martius, who hath done"
> *The Roman hero presents himself to his former enemy as an ally.*

V.iii.95–126,132–174. Volumnia: "Should we be silent and not speak"*
> *Coriolanus' mother comes to beg him to spare Rome for the sake of his family.*

INTIMATE SCENE SUGGESTIONS
II.i. *The tribunes Sicinius and Brutus plot against the proud Coriolanus.**
IV.iii. *Two spies, Nicanor and Adrian, casually discuss their trade.*

IV.v. *Coriolanus makes common cause with his former enemy, Aufidius, against the ungrateful city that has banished him.*

Public Scene Suggestions
I.x. *Though he hates crowds, Martius receives from Cominius his cognomen, Coriolanus, for his victory at Corioli.*
V.iii. *Coriolanus' mother, Volumnia, pleads on her knees for her son to spare Rome.**

Timon of Athens (c. 1605)
Timon of Athens is, most scholars think, an unfinished play. It appears to have been written collaboratively, perhaps with Middleton, but the script's loose ends were never tied up. There is no record of any performance of *Timon of Athens* in Shakespeare's time. This play is the least frequently performed of all of Shakespeare's canon, almost always in a liberal adaptation that attempts to mend some of the less satisfactory passages.

The play tells a simple story: Timon is the most generous of men but turns into a great hater of all humankind when his friends desert him in his time of need. For the first half of the play, Timon is seen giving lavish banquets and entertaining society. In the latter half, he has moved to a cave, where he insults and humiliates visitors until he withdraws from life completely, apparently burying himself.

Because of its generally unfinished state, it has less extractable material, but one early scene and two scenes near the play's end (one of which is extremely comic in tone) are widely admired.

Monologue Suggestion
IV.i.1–41. Timon: "Let me look back upon thee."
Timon curses Athens, as colorfully and bitterly as is imaginable.

Intimate Scene Suggestions
II.ii. *Timon finds out from his servant that his generosity has bankrupted him.*
IV.iii. *Timon argues with another misanthrope, Apemantus, about whose hatred of humankind is purer.*
IV.iii. *Flavius, Timon's former servant, finds his cave and reminds him that not all men are as bad as Timon believes.*

Ben Jonson (1572–1637)

Ben Jonson was one of the foremost comic writers of the period, and his career is discussed at length in chapter 1, along with selections from several plays. However, Jonson also had a wide knowledge of the classical writers and strong political views, so perhaps it is not surprising that he turned to classical history for two tragic plays. *Sejanus* failed when it was first performed at The Globe, perhaps for its unrelieved cynicism, and Jonson was once again prosecuted by the Privy Council, which investigated the contemporary "applications" of this darkly political play.

The title characters of both *Sejanus* and *Catiline* are more like Coriolanus or the ambitious anti-heroes of Marlowe than the sympathetic tragic figures of Brutus and Antony. Each is a conspirator who places his personal gain over that of the Roman state. Sejanus, who has flattered himself into the favor of Tiberius Caesar, uses this seeming protection to get away with seduction, murder, and conspiracy. However, Tiberius secretly employs another favorite, Macro, to spy on Sejanus and to engineer his spectacular and gruesome downfall.

In the later play, Catiline, resentful of being passed over for honors, conspires with other dissatisfied Romans to wrest absolute power first through election and then, failing that, through force. A major section of the play consists of long orations as Cicero defends the senate against Catiline's ambitious ranting.

Sejanus (1603)
Monologue Suggestions

II.ii. Sejanus: "If this be not revenge, when I have done"
Sejanus imagines avenging the insults from Drusus by seducing his wife and poisoning him.

III.i. Silius: "Ay, take part. Reveal yourselves"
In the Senate, the war hero Silius rejects the charges of treason made against him by Sejanus and his followers.

III.ii. Tiberius: "We cannot but commend thy piety"
Tiberius deflects Sejanus' presumptuous suggestion that he should marry the noble widow Livia.

IV.i. Agrippina: "Is this the happiness of being born great?"
Agrippina bitterly resents the suspicions that Sejanus has cast on her and her sons, who are in the line of succession.

V.x. Terentius: "O you, whose minds are good"
   *In a gruesome report to the senators gathered at the Temple of
   Apollo, Terentius describes how Sejanus was killed and torn apart
   by mobs.*

SCENE SUGGESTION
I.ii. *Sejanus asks the physician Eudemus to provide him access to the lady
Livia.*

Catiline (c. 1611)
MONOLOGUE SUGGESTIONS
I.i. Catiline: "How, friends!/Think you that I would bid you grasp
the wind"
   *Catiline explains to his conspirators why conditions are favorable
   for them to act now, and proposes a horrible toast.*
III.iii. Catiline: "What ministers men must for practice use"
   *Catiline categorizes the people he must use in his climb to tyranni-
   cal power.*
IV.ii. Cicero: "Thou cam'st erewhile into this senate"
   *In one of several lengthy orations, Cicero denounces Catiline's
   crimes and plots.*
V.v. Catiline: "I never yet knew, soldiers, that in fight"
   Catiline urges his army to fight bravely in terrible circumstances.
V.vi. Petreius: "The straits and needs of Catiline being such"
   *Petreius reports to the Senate about Catiline's last battle and his
   "brave bad death."*

SCENE SUGGESTIONS
II.i. *In a light-hearted scene, Fulvia questions her maid Galla about the
lady Sempronia.*
II.i. *Fulvia persuades her lover, Curius, to disclose that Catiline will be
elected consul.*

Jacobean and Caroline Tragedies

Tragedy under James I and his successor, Charles I, continued to evolve,
exploring new motifs and styles as the culture of court and country

shifted. Dramatists clearly were looking for increasingly sensational material and began to explore not merely the blood taboos of murder and mutilation, but also the sexual taboos of incest, adultery, and rape. These situations gave rise to increasingly complex and passionate female characters (although they were still played by boy actors).

In the great tragedies by Webster, Middleton, and Ford, sexual decadence is merely one manifestation of the general corruption of society. Illicit relationships sometimes provide the only love or generosity of spirit in otherwise cynical worlds, as in the secret marriage between the Duchess of Malfi and her steward or the incestuous affair between Giovanni and his sister Annabella in 'Tis Pity She's a Whore. Middleton's great tragedies use sexual misconduct as the route which ruins the heroines; the rape of Bianca in Women Beware Women drops her into a despairing cynicism, whereas Beatrice-Joanna in The Changeling learns that sex is a commodity like any other.

Actors have wonderful opportunities to create changing, growing characters in these complex plays. Be sure that you understand where a scene or monologue selection fits in your character's development over the course of the play.

Thomas Heywood (1574–1641)

The prolific and popular dramatist Thomas Heywood wrote in every genre. (His career is discussed at length in chapter 1.) Heywood's masterpiece is A Woman Killed with Kindness, a domestic tragedy about an ordinary English family. This in itself is something of a radical departure from earlier tragedy. Heywood's sensitive evocation of the cuckolded husband Frankford, his penitent wife Anne, and the lover Wendoll struggling between friendship and passion proves that the destruction of ordinary people is just as moving as that of a royal family. The absence of revenge is another fascinating departure from the adulterous tragedies of the period. Frankford ends his marriage calmly and civilly, like an adult trying to behave well, but the passion bottled up inside the characters leads inexorably to death.

A Woman Killed with Kindness (1603)
MONOLOGUE SUGGESTIONS

Scene 3. Sir Charles: "My God! what have I done? what have I done?"

Sir Charles repents killing two men in a fight over falconing.

Scene 6. Wendoll: "I am a villain if I apprehend"*
   Wendoll is tormented by his adulterous attraction for his friend Frankford's wife Anne.
Scene 6. Nicholas: "Zounds, I'll stab."
   Having seen Wendoll kissing his master's wife, the servant Nicholas plans to spy on them further.
Scene 13. Frankford: "This is the key that opes my outward gate"*
   Frankford cautiously approaches his bedroom, where he fears that he will find his wife and her lover.
Scene 13. Frankford: "My words are regist'red in Heaven already"✢
   Frankford expels his unfaithful wife from his home.

Scene Suggestions
Scene 6. *Wendoll confesses his love to Anne, his friend's wife.*
Scene 8. *Nicholas tells his master, Frankford, that his wife is unfaithful.*
Scene 14. *Sir Charles proposes to his sister, Susan, to pay his debt with her virginity.*

John Webster (c. 1580–c. 1637)
John Webster was perhaps the greatest tragedian of the generation after Shakespeare and Marlowe, although his works overlapped with Shakespeare's in the theaters. Webster's *The Duchess of Malfi* was in the repertory of the King's Men at the same time as *The Tempest,* for example. It is also one of the few plays of the period with a surviving cast list, which tells us exactly which actors played which parts. (Shakespeare had already retired from acting and was not part of the cast, but his famous friends Burbage, Condell, and Hemmings were.)

Like most of the other Jacobean dramatists, Webster began his career in collaboration with other playwrights; from 1602 to 1607, his name appears on half a dozen histories and city comedies. The little we know about Webster personally comes to us in the form of tributes and lampoons by his contemporaries. Although Webster was satirized for his pedantic, pompous demeanor, his two masterful tragedies, *The Duchess of Malfi* and *The White Devil,* were praised for their elegant dramatic poetry and compelling characterizations, which towered above the sensationalistic standards of the time. He is most admired for his horrifying and highly theatrical death scenes, in which heroes and villains are forced to come to terms with their pasts and the fact of their mortality.

The Duchess of Malfi (1614)
MONOLOGUE SUGGESTIONS
I.iii. Duchess: "The misery of us, that are born great"
   The Duchess urges Antonio to be confident of her love.
III.ii. Ferdinand: "The howling of a wolf / Is music to thee"
   Ferdinand curses his sister and her illicit husband.
III.v. Duchess: "I prithee, who is greatest? Can you tell?"
   *The Duchess argues that an individual's moral quality matters
   more than social rank.*
IV.ii. Ferdinand: "She and I were twins:"*
   Ferdinand mourns the Duchess, his murdered sister.

SCENE SUGGESTIONS
I.iii. *The widowed Duchess proposes marriage to her socially inferior secretary, Antonio, despite her brothers' objections.*
II.v. *The Duchess' brothers, Ferdinand and the Cardinal, rage that their sister is pregnant.*
IV.i. *The evil Bosola, at the instigation of the Duchess' brother, terrifies the Duchess.*
IV.ii. *The Duchess and her devoted attendant, Cariola, await death in prison.*
V.ii. *Bosola asks the seductive Julia to do him a favor.*
V.ii. *Julia discovers the secret that is troubling the Cardinal.*

The White Devil (1612)
MONOLOGUE SUGGESTIONS
IV.i. Francisco de Medici: "I gather now by this, some cunning fellow"
   The Duke sees his sister Isabella's ghost as he plans to avenge her death.
IV.ii. Vittoria: "What have I gain'd by thee but infamy?"
   Vittoria accuses her lover Bracciano of ruining her.
V.iv. Flamineo: "This night I'll know the utmost of my fate"
   The guilty Flamineo sees Bracciano's ghost and prepares to die.

SCENE SUGGESTIONS
I.ii. *Flamineo teases his jealous brother-in-law Camillo.*
II.i. *Bracciano rejects his wife Isabella, who has just arrived in Rome.*

Thomas Middleton

Middleton began his career by contributing to comedies for Philip Henslowe and became the master of "citizen comedy." Middleton's biography and selections from his comedies can be found in chapter 1.

During the 1610s and 1620s, Middleton's satire grew darker, and he began to write tragicomedies and tragedies. A curious tragicomedy, *The Witch,* may be of interest to Shakespeare students because it contains material that was somehow incorporated into the witches' scenes of *Macbeth.* Middleton enjoyed enormous popular success with a topical political satire, *A Game at Chess* (1624), which rendered the Spanish Catholics as the wicked black chess pieces and the English Protestants as the virtuous, victorious white pieces. With William Rowley he co-authored several plays, including *The Changeling,* one of the most popular of the Jacobean tragedies. The title refers to the "bed-trick" in which one woman replaces another in the dark bedroom, a device used in Shakespeare's *All's Well That Ends Well* and *Measure for Measure.* In *The Changeling,* the trick perpetuates the wicked career of Beatrice-Joanna, the tragic heroine who falls from privilege into murder and deceit. In Middleton's *Women Beware Women* (c. 1621), Bianca, another privileged woman, is tainted by the world of adultery, incest, rape, and murder in which she finds herself. The irony Middleton uses to such hilarious effect in the city comedies becomes deeply unsettling in the tragedies, in which a corrupt world no longer seems cause for laughter. Another important Jacobean work, *The Revenger's Tragedy,* has often been attributed to Middleton for its vicious irony (see the section on Tourneur).

Women Beware Women (c. 1621)
MONOLOGUE SUGGESTIONS
I.i. Leantio: "Speak low, sweet mother; you are able to spoil as many"
   The young husband urges his mother not to encourage his new bride to wish for things they can't afford.
I.ii. Isabella: "Marry a fool!/Can there be greater misery"
   Isabella is appalled at the wealthy idiot her father has arranged for her to marry.
II.ii. Bianca: "Now bless me from a blasting! I saw that now"
   Bianca curses Guardiano, who set up the situation for the Duke to rape her.

III.ii. Leantio: "Is she my wife till death, yet no more mine?"
Realizing that his wife Bianca has been corrupted, Leantio wonders how to go on with his marriage.

IV.iii. Bianca: "Sir, I have read you over all this while"
Bianca argues with the Cardinal for the possibility of converting sin into virtue.

SCENE SUGGESTIONS

II.i. *Livia deceives her niece Isabella about her real father so that Isabella will accept the (incestuous) suit of Livia's brother Hippolito.*

IV.i. *Leantio visits his estranged wife Bianca at the Duke's court.*

The Changeling (written with William Rowley) (c.1622)
MONOLOGUE SUGGESTIONS

II.i. De Flores: "Yonder's she."
De Flores fears that the beautiful Beatrice will scorn him for his appearance.

III.iv. De Flores: ". . . I have eased you/Of your trouble; think on't. I'm in pain"*
De Flores rejects Beatrice's gold and asked to be repaid in her bed.

IV.i. Beatrice: "This fellow has undone me endlessly"
Beatrice fears her bridegroom will discover on their wedding night that she is no longer a virgin.

SCENE SUGGESTIONS

II.i. *Beatrice and her servant De Flores explore their strange sexual attraction.*

II.ii. *Beatrice hires De Flores to poison her unwelcome suitor, Alonzo.*

III.iv. *De Flores pressures Beatrice to reward his service with her virginity.*

The Witch (1615)
MONOLOGUE SUGGESTIONS

I.ii. Hecate: "Thy boldness takes me bravely. We're all sworn"*
The witch anticipates what Sebastian might want her to perform.

I.ii. Sebastian: "Heaven knows with what unwillingness and hate"
Sebastian enters the witches' lair seeking revenge on his faithless lover, who has married another man.

II.i. Francisca: "I have the hardest fortune, I think of a hundred gentlewomen"
The unmarried Francisca rues her pregnancy.

II.ii. Almachildes: "What a mad toy took me to sup with witches"
  The "fantastical" and hung over Almachildes reviews the charms the witches gave him.

John Ford (1586–after 1639)

John Ford was one of the only professional playwrights of the English Renaissance to come from the gentry, and his career reflects his privileged position. He entered the Middle Temple of the Inns of Court at age sixteen, where he practiced law for many years. He dedicated his early poems and prose works to significant noble patrons. Most of his plays, both collaborations and solo works, were performed in private theaters.

His dramatic career began with collaborations with such prominent writers as Middleton, Webster, and Dekker. Following the accession of Charles I in 1625, Ford began to publish his independent works. Like many of the dramatists who were writing in the two decades after Shakespeare's death, Ford wrote dark and bizarre tales of obsessive passion and the dangerous ways it combines with politics. Ford's best-known tragedy, *'Tis Pity She's a Whore*, transforms a story of trapped young lovers similar to *Romeo and Juliet* into an incestuous romance between brother and sister within a corrupt Italian court. This compelling play is frequently revived on the modern stage, and its ambiguous moral dialectic continues to fuel critical debate. *The Broken Heart*, set in ancient Sparta, considers the tragedy of individuals opposing the inexorable social order; Ford's powerless female characters are particularly poignant in their vulnerability to a patriarchal destiny.

'Tis Pity She's a Whore (c. 1626–1633)

MONOLOGUE SUGGESTIONS

I.ii. Giovanni: "Lost, I am lost. My fates have doomed my death."
  Giovanni feels he is dying from his suppressed, illicit love for his sister.
I.ii. Putana: "How like you this, child?"*
  The bawdy governess considers the merits of Annabella's various suitors.
II.ii. Hippolita: "'Tis I: Do you know me now?"*
  Hippolita accuses her former lover, Soranzo, of abandoning her since her husband's recent death.
III.vi. Friar: "I am glad to see this penance; for believe me"
  The Friar warns Annabella of the torments of hell that await incestuous lovers.

V.i. Annabella: "Pleasures, farewell, and all ye thriftless minutes"
Annabella reflects on her tragic position.

SCENE SUGGESTIONS

I.ii. *Giovanni and his sister Annabella confront their incestuous desires.*
IV.iii. *Soranzo accuses his new bride, Annabella, of being a pregnant whore.*
IV.iii. *Soranzo's servant, Vasquez, coaxes Putana to tell him the name of Annabella's lover.*

The Broken Heart (c. 1629–1633)
MONOLOGUE SUGGESTION

II.i. Bassanes: "I'll have that window next the street dammed up"*
The jealous Bassanes fears any opportunity for his wife Penthea to deceive him.

SCENE SUGGESTIONS

II.iii. *The disguised Orgilus confronts his beloved Penthea, who is now unhappily married to another man.*
III.ii. *Penthea accuses her brother Ithocles of ruining her happiness.*
III.v. *Penthea describes her brother's merits and promotes his suit to the Princess Calantha.*

3   Histories

Histories by Shakespeare

If Shakespeare was not the inventor of this genre, then he was certainly one of its earliest and most prolific practitioners. Shakespeare's history plays dramatize the events of a lifetime of an English king. They are often sweeping looks at the era, with large numbers of characters and locations, rather than specifically biographical pieces about the kings themselves. The scale of these pieces is extremely large, even by the standards of early modern drama. They are based on actual events in English history, though Shakespeare was more than willing to make changes for dramatic effect, and his sources were not always unbiased.

These plays can be intimidating, even to the experienced reader. Not only are there a lot of characters, but many of them have the same names: Edwards and Richards proliferate. Confusingly, individual characters are variously identified by the title they hold, their family name, their first name, and a nickname. Characters may appear in more than one play (sometimes with changing names reflecting changing social status) or may be succeeded by later generations with the same names and titles.

To help sort out this puzzle, this chapter is organized chronologically according to the events portrayed. Eight of the ten history plays are loosely organized into a gigantic series covering the consecutive reigns of six kings. (Of the two other plays, one covers events occurring well before those of the main series and the other covers events that took place slightly later.) Shakespeare did not write the plays in this order, but for readers lacking the detailed knowledge of British history Shakespeare expected of his audience, this ordering can clarify the relationships and conflicts.

An Early Oddity
King John (c. 1590)

This play, covering the earliest events in history, is the most indeterminate in composition date but may have been the first one composed. The title character is King John (of the Robin Hood legends and the Magna Carta), who held the English throne from 1199 to 1216. The largest and most interesting character of the play, however, is the Bastard, Philip Falconbridge, who would himself be a claimant to the throne through his father, King Richard the Lionhearted, were it not for his illegitimate birth.

The events of the play mostly concern John's small-minded attempts to hold onto his throne against the rival claim of his nephew, Arthur, and the general erosion of his holdings in France. The play's tone is difficult to catch, but overall treats the wimpy king and his petty politics satirically. The death of Arthur and his mother's mourning provide a pathetic counterpoint, while the Bastard's sardonic asides give the play comedic lift.

King John has never been particularly popular, in part because the story is neither instructive nor tragic. John's death by poisoning (which is historically inaccurate but seems poetically just) is ignominious rather than heroic. However, Deborah Warner's 1988 production for the Royal Shakespeare Company revealed many of the play's theatrical merits. Because of the play's obscurity, there are many relatively unknown scenes and speeches, which may work powerfully when excerpted.

MONOLOGUE SUGGESTIONS

II.i.563–599. Bastard: "Mad world! Mad kings! Mad composition"
In narrative fashion, the Bastard expresses incredulity at events.

II.ii.1–26. Constance: "Gone to be married? Gone to swear a peace?"
   Arthur's mother discovers the French king has betrayed them.
III.iv.93–105. Constance: "Grief fills the room up of my absent child"
   While delivering her short, heart-wrenching speech of sorrow,
   Constance unbinds her hair as a symbol of her shattered psyche.
IV.i.41–58. Arthur: "Have you the heart?"
   The boy-prince appeals to his jailer not to carry out the orders to
   blind him.
V.vii.13–24. Prince Henry: "O, vanity of sickness! Fierce extremes"
   The young prince faces the imminent death of his father.
V.vii.70–79, 110–118. Bastard: "Art thou gone so? I do but stay be-
hind"
   The Bastard's two final speeches offering a stirring (if ironic) view of
   English unity.

Intimate Scene Suggestions

III.iii. *King John extracts a promise from a henchmen, Hubert, to murder*
the young prince.
IV.i. *The imprisoned Prince Arthur successfully pleads with his keeper,*
Hubert, for his life.
IV.ii. *To his temporary relief, King John hears that Hubert did not carry*
out his order to execute the prince.

The First Tetralogy
Richard II (c. 1595)
The historical Richard II came to the throne at the age of eleven and
ruled from 1377 to 1399. In his youth, his uncles ran the country
for him and were reluctant to step away from power when Richard
attained his majority. He twice had to seize power that was rightfully
his from those who would "help" him. His bitter resentment of those
who had failed him and his dependence on inexperienced favorites
for advice led him into numerous political mistakes. Eventually,
Richard was overthrown by his cousin, Bolingbroke, and was murdered at the age of thirty-three.

Shakespeare's play has several remarkable features. First, it is
written entirely in verse, even scenes depicting simple country gar-
deners. Second, it contains longer average speeches than any play
in the canon. There is an extraordinary number of possible monologues from this play, which, surprisingly, are not often performed.

Finally, it has a brilliantly designed structure, which leads the reader (or audience member) to find Richard unsympathetic at first. For nearly half the play, we identify most strongly with his opponents. As the play proceeds, however, and Richard begins his painful fall from power, we begin to reverse our former opinion. By the play's end, Richard achieves tragic stature.

The play meditates on what makes a good king, the personal cost of assuming the burden of the kingship, and the pain caused to a country by a bad king. Subsequent history plays will reveal the cost a country pays for deposing one.

MONOLOGUE SUGGESTIONS

I.ii.9–37. Duchess of Gloucester: "Finds brotherhood in thee no sharper spur"
> *Eleanor tries to stir her brother-in-law, Gaunt, to revenge her husband's death.*

I.ii.44–74. Duchess of Gloucester: "Farewell, Old Gaunt"*
> *Having been refused once, the Duchess again tries to incite revenge.*

I.iii.148–167. Mowbray: "A heavy sentence, my most sovereign liege"
> *Upon hearing that he has been banished, Mowbray relates his fears of living where no one can speak his language.*

II.i.31–68. John of Gaunt: "Methinks I am a prophet new inspired"
> *Often seen as a patriotic hymn, this speech actually dwells on the rottenness within the fortress as well as its inspiring exterior.*

III.ii.1–26. Richard II: "Harlechly Castle call they this at hand?"*
> *Glad to be on his own land again, the King delivers this speech to the land itself.*

III.ii.32–58. Richard II: "Discomfortable cousin, know'st thou not"
> *Hearing of his danger, the King invokes heaven as his partner in the fight.*

III.ii.140–174. Richard II: "No matter where. Of comfort no man speak."
> *Realizing the seriousness of his danger, the King goes into a dramatic lamentation.*

III.iii.30–66. Bolingbroke: "Go to the rude ribs of that ancient castle"
> *The King's usurping cousin returns from exile.*

IV.i.153–212. Richard II: "Alack, why am I sent for to a king"*
> *The King turns his deposition into a ceremony of "uninvestiture."*

V.ii.98–117. Duchess of York: "Why, York, what wilt thou do?"*
   The Duchess pleads with her husband not to betray their treasonous son's plot against the new king.

INTIMATE SCENE SUGGESTIONS

I.iii. *Bolingbroke is banished by the King, and his father, John of Gaunt, tries to comfort him.*
II.iii. *York, the acting Regent, unsuccessfully tries to calm the rebellious Bolingbroke.*

PUBLIC SCENE SUGGESTION

V.i. *The Queen says good-bye to her husband on his way to prison and death.*

Henry IV, Part I (c. 1596)

Written shortly after *Richard II*, this play is clearly intended to relate to it. It is not a sequel but a free-standing piece that looks at many of the same themes but from the opposite perspective. King Henry IV is, of course, Bolingbroke. This play shows us this capable but guilt-ridden king wrestling with his conscience. He has overthrown a legitimate king, and even though he was closely related to Richard, he was not the next in line for the throne. The play dramatizes the King's difficulty in establishing his authority against numerous rebellions. Owen Glendower rises in Wales, and the Percy family leads dissent in the North. Henry Percy has a close relationship with his son of the same name, who is known by his nickname, Hotspur.

The closeness of the Percy family is carefully contrasted with the King's estrangement from his own son, Prince Hal, a youth rebelling against his father's yoke. The scenes in which Hal interacts with his disreputable companions in the tavern alternate with those set in the stuffy court, giving this play a surprising texture. The movement between the highest and lowest levels of society creates an exceptionally detailed and complete world for this play, in comparison to the confined and elevated worlds of many of the other histories.

Many find Hal's surrogate father at the tavern, Sir John Falstaff, the most original and appealing character in the play. Thanks in part to his presence, Hal's scenes eventually come to dominate the play. The education of Hal climaxes when he must face his foil, Hotspur, in battle.

Since Shakespeare's time, this has been among the most popular of the histories. The extractable material from it is brilliant and challenging, but also well known. It is, for this reason, slightly more useful in the classroom than in auditions.

MONOLOGUE SUGGESTIONS

I.i.1–46. King Henry IV: "So shaken as we are, so wan with care"
Bolingbroke, now king, suffers from his guilt and the burdens of the throne.

I.ii.173–195. Prince Hal: "I know you all, and will a while uphold"
Though generally thought irresponsible, the Prince reveals his true nature.

I.iii.28–68. Hotspur: "My liege, I did deny no prisoners"
The hot-headed nobleman defends his failure to cooperate with the King.

II.iv.31–58. Lady Percy: "O my good lord, why are you thus alone?"
Hotspur's wife seeks both to calm him and to charm his secret from him.

II.v.363–382. Falstaff: "Peace, good pint-pot; peace, good tickle-brain"
The drunken Falstaff pretends to be the King for Prince Hal's benefit.

III.ii.129–159. Prince Hal: "Do not think so; you shall not find it so."
Hal pledges his loyalty to the King and swears he will fight and defeat Hotspur.

V.i.127–139. Falstaff: "'Tis not due yet."
Falstaff's famous speech on honor.

INTIMATE SCENE SUGGESTIONS

I.ii. *Prince Hal good-naturedly ribs his fat companion, Falstaff.*
I.iii. *Young, angry Hotspur and his cooler uncle, Worcester, plan a rebellion.*
II.iii. *Hotspur hides the rebellion from his wife, who is hurt but finally accepts his secrecy.*

PUBLIC SCENE SUGGESTION

II.iv. *In the play's most famous scene, Hal and Falstaff imitate and mock the King.*

Henry IV, Part 2 (c. 1596)

The relationship of the two parts of *Henry IV* is unclear. The play may have been originally written as one work, which was later divided into two parts because it was too long. Or Part 2 may have been planned as a sequel, when Shakespeare realized that Part 1 defers rather than resolves its conflicts. In any case, Part 2 is not really independent of the more self-contained, but incomplete, Part 1 and is most often performed in an edited combination with it. Part 2 continues the story of the first play, again largely focusing on the King's troubled conscience and equally troubled relationship to his son, Prince Hal. The death-bed reconciliation of father and son forms the hopeful finish to this piece.

MONOLOGUE SUGGESTIONS

Induction.1–40. Rumor: "Open your ears; for which of you will stop"
   The personification of rumor delivers this prologue to the play.
II.i.78–94. Mistress Quickly: "Marry, if thou wert an honest man"
   Quickly is furious at Falstaff, because he has promised, but failed, to marry her.
II.iii.9–44. Lady Percy: "O yet, for God's sake, go not to these wars!"
   Hotspur's widow pleads with her father-in-law to cease his rebellion against the King.
III.i.4–31. King Henry IV: "How many thousand of my poor subjects"
   In a quiet, midnight soliloquy, the King reflects on his burdens.
IV.iii.79–111. Falstaff: "I would you had but the wit; 'twere better than your dukedom. Good faith, this same young sober blooded boy . . ."
   Falstaff celebrates drink and drinking in a speech to Prince Hal's younger brother.
IV.iii.151–177. Prince Hal: "Why doth the crown lie there upon his pillow"
   Gazing on the crown, Hal (incorrectly thinking his father dead) assumes the kingship.
V.v.45–69. Prince Hal (now King Henry V): "I know thee not, old man. Fall to thy prayers"
   Firmly, the new king rejects his former wild companion, Falstaff.

INTIMATE SCENE SUGGESTIONS

I.ii. *Falstaff is warned to stay away from the Prince by the lord chief justice of London.*
II.ii. *The Prince and his friend, Poins, compare their places in the world.*
III.ii. *Two old men, Justices Silence and Shallow, recall better days.*
IV.iv. *The reconciliation scene between the King and his heir.*

Henry V (c. 1599)

Because of Kenneth Branagh's film, this history play is enjoying a current popularity. In this play, Prince Hal, now sitting on the throne as Henry V, proves himself an able king and ruler despite his reprobate youth. Here the emphasis is on external conflict with France, rather than on internal rebellions. The king leads a campaign to claim land in France to which he has a legitimate, if obscure, claim. His small army is heavily outnumbered and afraid. Harry passes among them in disguise the night before battle and learns firsthand of their opinions of him. He courageously leads them in battle against the overwhelming opposition and carries the day.

After the battle, the King's wooing of the French princess offers comic counterpoint to what has gone before. The successful arrangement for a marriage ends the conflict and caps the so-called first tetralogy with an upbeat ending.

The great battlefield orations of this play are superior pieces of rhetoric, even if they are received more dubiously in our time. The scenes involving Princess Catherine are written in French, a daring risk for a playwright to take. The speeches of the Chorus, however, invoking the audience's imagination, are the most innovative sections of the play.

MONOLOGUE SUGGESTIONS

Prologue.1–34. Chorus: "O for a muse of fire that would ascend"
   The opening speech of the play.

II.iii.9–23. Mistress Quickly: "Nay, sure he is not in hell."
   In her only appearance in this play, Quickly describes Falstaff's death.

III.o.1–35. Chorus: "Thus with imagined wing our swift scene flies"
   In the introduction to the third act, the Chorus describes the English preparations for war.

III.i.1–34. King Henry V: "Once more into the breach, dear friends, once more"
   The king urges his troops to sustain their attack on the walls of Harfleur.

III.ii.27–49. Boy: "As young as I am, I have observed"
   In a great speech for a child actor, the boy reveals his honesty amidst corruption and sloth.

IV.i.212–266. King Henry V: "Upon the King."
   Shaken from his disguised encounter with his men, the King reflects on his responsibilities.

IV.iii.18–67. King Henry V: "What's he that wishes so."
This famous charge to the troops is known as the "St. Crispin's day" speech. Its familiarity makes it challenging to make fresh, but the speech is so well constructed that it is a joy to rehearse and perform.

INTIMATE SCENE SUGGESTIONS
III.iv. *The French lady-in-waiting, Alice, attempts to teach the Princess English.*
V.i. *Captain Gower and the Welsh captain, Fluellen, force the obnoxious Pistol to eat a leek.*
V.ii. *In his own awkward and endearing way, King Henry woos the princess.*

PUBLIC SCENE SUGGESTION
IV.i. *In disguise the night before the battle, Henry engages the soldier Williams on the subject of leaders and followers.*

The Second Tetralogy
The second tetralogy (which was actually written well before the plays covering the earlier period) chronicles England's War of the Roses, a civil war that was in many ways a huge family feud between the closely related Houses of York and Lancaster over control of the English throne. The four plays that comprise it are now known as *Henry VI, Parts 1, 2,* and *3,* and *Richard III,* but only the last of these was originally performed under the title we now use. The play we now call *1 Henry VI,* in fact, was written after Parts 2 and 3. It is a "prequel," filling in background previously uncovered.

Written early in Shakespeare's career, when they were apparently quite popular, the *Henry VI* plays have had little stage success until the second half of the twentieth century. Recently, they have been revived in heavily edited and combined versions that have had highly successful runs, such as Peter Hall and John Barton's version, called *The War of the Roses,* and Adrian Noble's condensation, called *The Plantagenets.*

Henry VI, Part I (c. 1592)
1 Henry VI opens with the funeral of Henry V, who died suddenly, leaving an infant son as heir. The play covers nearly two decades, from the King's infancy to early adulthood, so the King himself is able to take a part in the action before the end of the play, but he is

far from being the central character. The strongest character is the heroic Lord Talbot, "the scourge of the French," who fights valiantly to hold onto the English lands in France won by Henry V. Talbot is contrasted with the infant Henry's squabbling uncles, Humphrey, Duke of Gloucester, and Henry Beaufort, Bishop of Winchester, by his desire to serve country rather than self. His enemy is Joan La Pucelle, the woman we now know as Joan of Arc. First-time readers are often shocked that Shakespeare does not share our saintly vision of Joan. He portrays her as a lying witch and whore, though in ways that are theatrically invigorating. She is a refreshing character, if a villainous one.

In some of the play's best scenes, Suffolk woos Margaret of Anjou on behalf of the King. Pious Henry has agreed to marry her, without ever having seen her, in hopes that it will create peace between England and France. Suffolk has agreed to court her because he intends to make her his mistress. Margaret is a character that will appear in all the plays of the tetralogy, a great tour-de-force in combined versions of the plays.

A particularly famous scene is the so-called temple garden scene, in which followers of the Houses of York and Lancaster pluck red or white roses to symbolize their loyalties.

MONOLOGUE SUGGESTIONS

I.iii.51–71. Joan La Pucelle: "Dauphin, I am by birth a shepherd's daughter"
   Joan relates her visions to the French crown prince.
I.vii.19–39. Talbot: "My thoughts are whirled like a potter's wheel"
   The great warrior of England is confused as he loses a battle unexpectedly.
III.vii.44–84. Joan La Pucelle: "Look on my country, look on fertile France"*
   Joan convinces the Duke of Burgundy to stay in the battle on France's side.
V.iii.1–29. Joan: "The Regent conquers, and the Frenchmen fly."
   Joan tries witchcraft to avoid capture, but her powers fail her.
V.vi.36–53. Joan: "First, let me tell you whom you have condemned"
   Lying through her teeth, Joan pleads high birth to escape her fate. It doesn't work.

INTIMATE SCENE SUGGESTIONS

I.iii. *By defeating him at sword play, Joan convinces the French Dauphin, Charles, that she is worthy to lead his troops.*

II.iii. *The Countess of Auvergne thinks she has captured Talbot through trickery but discovers he is less trusting than she had planned.*

IV.v. *John finds his dying father, Talbot, on the battlefield and dies himself of a broken heart.*

V.iii. *Suffolk woos Margaret for the King, and perhaps for himself, too.*

Henry VI, Part 2 (c. 1590)

Originally known by the enormous title, *The First Part of the Contention betwixt the Two Famous Houses of York and Lancaster, with the death of the good Duke Humphrey and the banishment and death of the Duke of Suffolk, and the tragical end of the proud Cardinal of Winchester, with the notable rebellion of Jack Cade, and the Duke of York's first claim unto the crown,* this play contains all this and more.

Suffolk lays a plot to entrap the Duchess of Gloucester and her husband, Humphrey, which succeeds when the Duchess traffics with witchcraft to see the future. As a consequence, she is banished, and her innocent, uninvolved husband is publicly disgraced, which leads to his death. However, a popular uprising protesting good Duke Humphrey's death leads directly to Suffolk's downfall and death. Such ironic turns of fate are common in this play. The Duke of York's pawn, Jack Cade, for example, leads a popular rebellion that turns against York in the end.

As in Part 1, Henry VI is a much smaller role than those of kings in the other histories. The original title clearly indicates that the play was designed to be more about the times than the man. Nonetheless, King Henry is an interesting figure, a pious and deeply spiritual man, who is ineffectual as a ruler and as a husband. He wishes to be left alone in his privacy, a luxury not afforded to kings then any more than it is now.

The play is notable for the prominent roles given to women and for the amount of time dedicated to common men. Substantial amounts of prose in the play give it verbal variety.

MONOLOGUE SUGGESTIONS

I.ii.1–16. Eleanor, Duchess of Gloucester: "Why droops my lord, like overripened corn?"

Eleanor scolds her husband for his lack of ambition.

I.ii.87–107. Hume: "Hume must make merry with the Duchess' gold"
A corrupt priest rejoices that he has tricked the Duchess out of her money.

I.iii.46–91. Margaret: "My lord of Suffolk, say, is this the guise?"*
The new Queen quickly sizes up the whole court and shows that she is a force to be reckoned with.

II.iv.20–58. Eleanor: "Come you, my lord, to see my open shame?"*
Paraded through the streets for her crimes, Eleanor bemoans her fallen state.

III.i.4–41. Queen Margaret: "Can you not see, or will ye not observe"
Margaret arranges the downfall of good Duke Humphrey.

IV.i.71–103. Captain: "Pole/Ay, kennel, puddle, sink, whose filth and dirt"*
Finding that Suffolk is his prisoner, the Captain tells him he will be executed for his crimes against good Duke Humphrey and the state.

IV.vii.1–2, 11–12, 20–39. Jack Cade: "So, sirs: Now go some and pull down the Savoy"*
A commoner leads a rebellion that is already spiraling out of his control.

V.iii.31–65. Young Clifford: "Shame and confusion! All is on the rout!"
Finding his slain father, Clifford both mourns and swears revenge.

INTIMATE SCENE SUGGESTIONS

I.ii. *The Duke of Gloucester and his wife cautiously reveal their ambitions to each other.*

I.iii. *Queen Margaret swears to her banished lover, Suffolk, that she will see him again.*

IV.x. *The starving Jack Cade breaks into the garden of Iden, for which he is killed.*

Henry VI, Part 3 (c. 1591)

Richard, Duke of York is the alternate title of *3 Henry VI*, but neither adequately suggests the play's intricate plot. In it, King Henry VI agrees to grant succession to Richard, Duke of York, rather than his own son, in recognition that his title was inherited through the usurping Henry IV. Queen Margaret will have none of this compromise, which displaces her son, Prince Edward. She sidelines her husband, who is not much help in battle, and leads the forces that capture York, whom she taunts and then orders killed.

The new Duke of York, Richard's son Edward, soon leads revenging forces to capture King Henry and imprison him. Margaret flees with her son to France, where it looks like she has been outmaneuvered. Edward, who has crowned himself Edward IV, sends his ally, Warwick, ahead to strike a deal with the French king. The deal falls through when Edward's marriage makes him unavailable for a match with a princess of France. Warwick defects and returns to England to capture Edward and restore Henry to the throne. Edward escapes his imprisonment to face down Margaret at Tewkesbury, where she and the young prince are captured. The Prince is killed, and Edward's brother, Richard, who will become Richard III, is only stopped at the last minute from killing Margaret, too. Instead, he slips off to the Tower, where Henry has been reimprisoned, and kills him.

The crown changes hands (or heads?) three times in the course of the play, and the final speech by Richard, Duke of Gloucester, tells us he plans to see it change again soon.

The bombastic verse of this play is great audition material, and the extractable scenes in it are only rarely performed.

MONOLOGUE SUGGESTIONS

I.iv.67–109. Margaret: "Brave warriors, Clifford and Northumberland"
Sadistically, the Queen mocks the captured rebel York, whose execution she orders at the end of the speech.

II.v.1–54. King Henry VI: "This battle fares like to the morning war"
The King steps aside from the battle, where he is useless, and contemplates the simple life.

II.vi.1–30. Clifford: "Here burns my candle out—Ay, here it dies"
Severely wounded, Clifford delivers his death speech.

III.ii.124–195. Richard Gloucester: "Ay, Edward will use women honorably"
In the longest uninterrupted speech in the canon, Richard plans to seize the crown.

V.iv.1–38. Queen Margaret: "Great Lords, wise men ne'er sit and wail their loss"
On the run, Margaret rallies (and threatens) her remaining supporters.

V.vi.61–94. Richard Gloucester: "What—will the aspiring blood of Lancaster"

> *Immediately upon killing King Henry, Richard swears that he will kill more to become king himself.*

INTIMATE SCENE SUGGESTIONS

III.ii. *Lady Anne Grey declines to become King Edward's mistress but accepts his offer of marriage.*

V.vi. *Richard Gloucester begins his rise to become Richard III by murdering Henry VI.*

Richard III (c. 1593)

The final play in the War of the Roses tetralogy is dominated by its fascinating, repellent central figure. The character of Richard is often said to be the character actor's Hamlet, in a play that is second only to *Hamlet* in length. Richard is, simultaneously, charming and utterly evil. He schemes for the crown, indifferent to the fact that his brothers now stand in the way, not the hated Lancasters. He successfully seduces the widow of Prince Edward, virtually on top of the coffin of her father-in-law, Henry VI. He lives outrageously and dies ignominiously.

Richard III can be difficult to read and perform, as it is clearly meant as the end of a series, and it expects the audience to be familiar with the previous history. Characters who lived and died in earlier plays are named and mourned. Clever editing, often incorporating scenes from the *Henry VI* series, is common in contemporary productions.

Despite this difficulty, the plot is straightforward and generally clear. Richard manipulates his way into the crown but finds it impossible to hold. His sins catch up with him, which he himself points out in his troubled soliloquies near the end of the play. His opponent is Richmond, soon to be Henry VII, the founder of the Tudor line to which Queen Elizabeth belonged. Partially flattering the contemporary mythology, Richmond is idealized as God's avenging angel on earth. His defeat of Richard restores peace to the land and ends the cycle of dissension begun with the deposition of Richard II nearly two hundred years earlier.

There are many rewarding roles in *Richard III* beyond the title character. Queen Margaret, who has played such an important role in the entire tetralogy, appears in this play to curse and taunt the king she hates so much. Other fine women's roles are Lady Anne, Queen Elizabeth, and the Duchess of York. Richard's allies, Hastings and Buckingham, are also sizable and nuanced roles.

MONOLOGUE SUGGESTIONS

I.i.1–40. Richard: "Now is the winter of our discontent"
An extremely famous speech, which sets up the entire play.

I.ii.1–32. Lady Anne: "Set down, set down your honorable load."
Lady Anne stops the funeral procession of her father-in-law to deliver a speech of mourning that turns into accusations against his murderer.

I.ii.43–65. Lady Anne: "What, do you tremble? Are you all afraid?"*
Facing the murderer himself, Anne portrays him as the devil, complete with unholy signs.

I.ii.215–250. Richard: "Was ever woman in this humor wooed?"
Astonished that his seduction of Anne worked, Richard revels in his villainy.

IV.iii.1–22. Tyrrell: "The tyrannous and bloody act is done"
In soliloquy, Tyrrell regrets his part in the murder of the two young princes.

IV.iv.82–123. Margaret: "I called thee then 'vain flourish of my fortune'."*
Henry VI's widow teaches the widow of Edward IV how to curse the hated Richard.

V.v.190–224. Richmond: "Why then, 'tis time to arm, and give direction."
In another very well-known speech, the man who will become Henry VII inspires his troops.

INTIMATE SCENE SUGGESTIONS

IV.ii. *Richard and Buckingham both realize that the other is untrustworthy.*
IV.iv. *Echoing the earlier seduction of Anne, Richard persuades Henry VI's widow to woo her daughter on his behalf.*

PUBLIC SCENE SUGGESTIONS

I.ii. *The famous funeral procession scene.*
III.vii. *Buckingham plays his part in a staged scene to get the public to beg a "reluctant" Richard to take the crown.*

One Last History
All Is True (Henry VIII) (with John Fletcher) (c. 1613)

The latest historical events formed the basis for the last history play that Shakespeare wrote, this time in collaboration with John Fletcher. Like the other history plays, it is often now known by the King's name rather than the original title used here.

All Is True treats events early in the reign of Henry VIII and ends with the climactic baptism of the infant Elizabeth, who was to become Queen for most of Shakespeare's life. Like many plays written late in Shakespeare's career, this one places a heavy emphasis on spectacle and a lesser one on character development.

Cardinal Wolsey is the tragic center of this play, a character who rises to greatness by helping his king dispense with an unwanted wife, only to be displaced from the King's inner circle by the new wife. The discarded Queen, Katherine, is also a beautifully written character whose retrospective speeches can be very rewarding to work on.

The play, overall, has not found favor since the mid-century. Its rather rigid pageantry is now unfashionable. However, All Is True has some interesting extractable moments that rise above the general level of the play.

MONOLOGUE SUGGESTIONS

II.iv.11–54. Queen Katherine: "Sir, I desire you do me right and justice"
The Queen defends herself with legal arguments in her divorce trial.
III.ii.351–373. Cardinal Wolsey: "So farewell—to the little good you bear me."
The Cardinal feels keenly his fall from power and wealth.

SCENE SUGGESTIONS

I.i. *The Lords Buckingham and Norfolk feel very differently about Cardinal Wolsey.*
II.iii. *Anne Boleyn claims she does not want to be Queen, but her old friend sees through her.*
IV.i. *Now fallen from power, Wolsey advises his secretary, Cromwell, to avoid his mistakes.*
IV.ii. *The old and ill ex-Queen Katherine seeks some resolution to her life in conversation with Griffith.*

Histories by Shakespeare's Contemporaries

No other dramatist produced as many history plays as Shakespeare. However, many playwrights of the age turned their hands to English history. From Peele's *Edward I* (1591) to Ford's *Perkin Warbeck* (1632), dramatists consulted the "chronicle histories" of Holinshed, Foxe, Stow, and Halle for dramatic material.

However, the inherent political content of the histories sometimes made them risky plays to present. All plays were censored by the Master of the Revels before they were produced, but occasionally plays were halted by higher authorities. In one famous instance, when the rebellious Earl of Essex had arranged a 1601 revival of *Richard II*, Queen Elizabeth drew the inevitable comparison, commenting, "I am Richard II. Know ye not that?"[1] James I and Charles I were even less patient with dramatic comparisons to previous rulers, and English history plays were few and far between after Elizabeth's death. (However, playwrights made full use of classical and foreign history to draw their political arguments.)

The two works discussed next come from the beginning and the end of the history play tradition. Both are by notable tragedians, who shaped historical events, as Shakespeare did, to serve their dramatic purposes.

Christopher Marlowe (1564–1593)

The great tragedian Christopher Marlowe wrote several plays based on historical sources. (His career is discussed in chapter 2.) *The Massacre at Paris* described the comparatively recent French history of the St. Bartholomew's Day massacre. In *Edward II*, Marlowe, like Shakespeare, turned to Holinshed's *Chronicles* for source material from English history.

This complex play traces the shifting alliances between the King, his favorite, Gaveston, the Queen, and the rebellious barons, led by Mortimer. *Edward II* raises the same political question as Shakespeare's *Richard II*: how may citizens deal with a bad king? In Marlowe's play, no figure holds moral authority; the king luxuriates in self-indulgence and is manipulated by his unscrupulous (homosexual?) favorites, but the barons and their allies in the Church are presented as rapacious and brutal.

The great twentieth-century dramatist Bertolt Brecht was fascinated by the political dilemmas that *Edward II* presents to its audience. Recent productions have often concentrated on the homosexual elements in the play and investigated the demonization of Edward's court.

Edward II (c. 1592)
MONOLOGUE SUGGESTIONS

I.i. Gaveston: "My father is deceas'd, come Gaveston"
    Gaveston relishes the opportunity to join the King in London.
I.iv. Queen Isabella: "Oh miserable and distressed queen!"
    Isabella envies the King's preference for Gaveston.
V.i. Edward: "Ah, Leicester, weigh how hardly I can brook"
    Edward muses on kingship and refuses to give up the crown.

INTIMATE SCENE SUGGESTIONS

I.iv. *The King parts from his favorite, Gaveston.*
V.v. *In an astonishing scene that feels more like a seduction than an assassination, Lightborn murders the deposed king.*

John Ford (1586–c. 1640)
Another tragedian, John Ford, turned to English history for material for *Perkin Warbeck*. This fascinating history play, written nearly forty years after Shakespeare's histories, dramatizes the challenge made by the title character to Henry VII and examines the monarch's claims to authority. Perkin Warbeck, who is clearly a pretender in Ford's play, gains support for his cause by appealing to King James of Scotland (ancestor to Charles, King of England during most of Ford's career). The Scottish are generous and supportive of Warbeck's cause and join with him in battle against the English, their customary enemy. In Scotland, Warbeck also meets and marries the virtuous Lady Katherine, who loves him and believes in his cause. Ford brings poignancy to the straightforward events of Warbeck's ruin by showing them through Katherine's eyes.

Perkin Warbeck (c. 1632)
MONOLOGUE SUGGESTIONS

I.ii. Katherine: "My worthiest lord and father, the indulgence"*
    The noble Katherine tactfully follows her father's advice and declines her young suitor's proposal.

II.i. Warbeck: "Most high, most mighty king!"
Warbeck presents himself as an ally to King James of Scotland.
III.i. Dawbney: "Briefly thus:/The Cornish under Audley disappointed"
Dawbney describes a suspenseful battle to King Henry.
III.iv. Durham: "Warlike King of Scotland"
The Bishop of Durham promises that battle will continue as long as Scotland recognizes Warbeck's claim to the English throne.
V.i. Katherine: "It is decreed; and we must yield to fate"*
Katherine mourns that in defeat she may not return to Scotland.

Scene Suggestion
III.ii. *Katherine asks to accompany her new husband, Warbeck, to the wars.*

Romances and Tragicomedies

The term *tragicomedy* means exactly what it sounds like, a combination of the two classical genres of tragedy and comedy. While there are classical examples of tragi-comedy, like Plautus' *Amphitryon* and various plays by Euripides, the early Renaissance critics preferred to ignore these and to insist that good plays were either tragic or comic. (Philostrate shares this view in *A Midsummer Night's Dream* when he turns up his nose at the "tragical mirth" of the rude mechanicals' "lamentable comedy" of Pyramus and Thisbe.) However, playwrights were eager to give opportunities for the popular actors of any troupe to perform the material that suited them best, and began inserting highly serious scenes into comedies and clownish scenes into tragedies. Some playwrights, like Beaumont and Fletcher, began to write plays that could no longer be identified by the old terms. When audiences began flocking to the dramatists' new mixed plays, the term *tragicomedy* was revived to describe them.

Typically, a tragicomedy progresses like a tragedy, in which the central characters go through harrowing circumstances that bring them close to death, but ends like a comedy, in which the characters ultimately resolve their difficulties satisfactorily, if not completely happily. As we have seen, many of the Jacobean plays by Shakespeare and his contemporaries fit this pattern perfectly, and some of the plays listed as "comedies" in the Folio and in this book could also be described as tragicomedies.

Although the plays known as "romances" contain this mixture of comic and tragic elements, they also share some unique qualities that set them apart from tragicomedies. A "romance" in the Renaissance did not imply a love story. Originally, it was a rather sprawling literary form like a novel, which carried its heroes and heroines through many picturesque settings and improbable circumstances far removed from everyday life. A romance might follow characters through many years and various locations, in events both pleasant and unpleasant. Romances tended to be episodic, picking up new characters and plot lines along the way and then discarding them; and they included many elements from folklore, such as ghosts, fairies, mystical predictions, and fantastic circumstances reuniting characters after prolonged separation and presumed death.

Several of the Elizabethan dramatists, including Greene, Lyly, and Lodge, wrote very popular prose romances. It is scarcely surprising, therefore, that the growing theater companies wanted to capitalize on this popularity by creating theatrical equivalents. (Shakespeare's As You Like It and The Winter's Tale were both adaptations of prose romances.) Eventually, a "romance" in the theater came to mean a play that included a series of episodes in various settings, usually with a wide range of characters (including figures from folklore), and a series of nonrealistic, often magical adventures.

The classically minded critics disapproved very strongly of the sprawling nature of the romances. In accordance with Greek and Roman precedents, they believed that good comedies or tragedies should take place in one setting, over the course of one fictional day. In 1616, playwright and critic Ben Jonson turned up his nose at "th'ill customs of the age," including the tendency of the romance playwrights "to make a child, now swaddled, to proceed/ Man, and then shoot up, in one beard and weed,/Past threescore years," or to employ a Chorus who "wafts you o'er the seas." Jonson preferred the realistic, everyday concerns of pure comedy. But the romances of Shakespeare and his colleagues have a special magic all their own.

Romances and Tragicomedies by Shakespeare

At the end of his writing career, Shakespeare wrote a series of plays that falls into the genre of tragicomedy. These plays are very similar in tone and in their thematic ideas. They use many repeating plot devices and motifs. In less intense forms, these ideas are present in some of Shakespeare's earlier comedies, and, in fact, these plays are classed as comedies in the *Folio*. Because they have special common characteristics, scholars have come to consider them separately, and have created a new name to signify their particular qualities. These plays have come to be known collectively as "the romances." Because the plays were written in a short span of time, they form a natural group with more similarities than any of the other genre categories, which contain plays written across the span of the writer's active professional life.

The romances employ motifs of loss and restoration, of youthful innocence offering hope for renewal to an older, traumatized generation, and of second chances to correct past mistakes. These stories have been cast into mythic rather than realistic formats and consciously employ highly unlikely, even miraculous endings.

The reception of these plays has varied more, across time, than any of Shakespeare's other plays. Excepting *The Tempest,* which has been held in high esteem almost continuously since its writing, these plays have been hard for later ages to place and understand. There have always been voices of appreciation, but just as often the plays have been discounted. Their conscious unreality and highly unlikely happy endings have sometimes been misunderstood as weak artistry. For example, many scholars supposed, until more precise dating information became available, that these works were very early plays, because it was presumed that the author had not yet figured out how to end his plays without miraculous intervention.

The critical esteem for the plays has climbed steadily throughout the 20th century, however. Particularly since the 1970s these works have been seen as profound in the way that fairytales and myths can be profound. They have a simplicity that conceals their depths.

For actors, these plays contain extreme challenges. The verse in them is especially convoluted, containing multiple uses of all of the patterns of variation. They challenge conventional ideas about characterization, because they require emotional intensity without necessarily implying realistic motivations. When well performed, their effect can seem magical, but it takes very practical means to achieve this effect. Clearly, these plays are the furthest from twentieth-century techniques, so the actors must bring original and unconventional thinking to their approaches. They are especially interesting and beautiful material.

Pericles (c. 1607)

The 1623 *Folio of Shakepeare's Works* did not contain this play. *Pericles* exists only in a garbled "bad" quarto, and we have no reason to think that a full, accurate version of it ever went into print. Unfortunately, the edition of the play we wish for will probably never be recovered.

We don't know why Shakespeare's colleagues didn't include *Pericles* in the *Folio,* though perhaps it is simply because there was not a good text available at printing time. Many scholars speculate that the play was written in collaboration with another author. Heminges and Condell may have left it out of the *Folio* because it was not, in their minds, Shakespeare's, though that hardly explains the reason why other jointly authored plays were included.

This play is, therefore, as problematic as *Timon of Athens,* but in a different way. *Pericles* was, we know from contemporary commentary and from its printing history, very popular in its own time. It was performed often and received enthusiastically. *Timon,* of course, has no record of performance at all, and it may have been abandoned in an unfinished state. *Pericles,* by contrast, clearly existed in a form other than the one we have now.

Even in its fractured form, however, *Pericles* is a powerful epic tale. It follows the voyages of the young Prince Pericles around the Mediterranean. After being shipwrecked on a foreign shore, he wins a tournament and thereby, a bride. He is again at sea, in the midst of a storm, when his wife dies (he thinks) in childbirth; Pericles sets her coffin adrift on the stormy waters after the hastiest of funerals. In his grief, and in the midst of travels, he leaves his newborn daughter, Marina, with foster parents and continues toward home.

The play then skips forward in time, to follow the adventures of the unfortunate daughter who is almost murdered, then kidnapped by pirates and sold into a brothel. Her steadfast virtue shames the customers into leaving her alone and builds her reputation as a remarkable person. Pericles, whose grief for his wife and now-lost daughter has frozen him into a deep, speechless depression, is brought to meet this mythically virtuous young woman in hopes that she can effect his cure. In a miraculous scene of restoration, Pericles realizes that the young woman is his daughter, Marina. Pericles recovers and is wondrously reunited with his wife, who did not die after all. (She washed ashore, where talented physicians recognized that she still lived, and was cured.) The Goddess Diana reveals her whereabouts to Pericles in a vision.

For those who know the other romances, it is easy to speculate that *Pericles* may have been among Shakespeare's finest works. Because of the textual problems, the play is now rarely performed, however, and almost always in heavily reworked editions that try to amend the areas of difficulty in the corrupted text.

The play, of course, presents vast challenges. The roles of Pericles and his wife require immense range, as they appear in the play first as a young couple and later as middle aged. (This is sometimes handled in performance by letting two different sets of actors play the two halves of the roles, but most performances eschew that for the virtuoso option of letting the actors show their range.) Other actors, especially those playing Marina and Diana, have the challenge of seeming celestial without stooping to parody.

MONOLOGUE SUGGESTIONS
Scene 1 (I.i). 164–185. Pericles: "How courtesy would seem to cover sin"

> *Pericles has "solved" the riddle of the King of Antioch but cannot reveal the answer because it places him in peril of his life. He contemplates his predicament.*

Scene 15 (IV.i). 53–81. Dionyza: "Thy oath remember. Thou hast sworn to do it."

> *The woman who has raised Marina orders her death.*

Scene 17 (IV.iii). 29–52. Dionyza: "Yet none does know but you how she came dead"*

> *Believing her orders carried out, Dionyza manipulates her husband to ensure his silence.*

INTIMATE SCENE SUGGESTIONS
Scene 17 (IV.iii). *Dionyza, the foster-mother of Pericles' daughter, confesses to her husband, Cleon, that she ordered the girl murdered because she outshone their own daughter.*
Scene 21 (V.i). *Pericles is restored to health by his dawning realization that he is in the presence of his long-lost daughter, Marina.*

Cymbeline

Like *All's Well That Ends Well*, this play draws on Boccaccio's *Decameron* for its source material. Again like *All's Well, Cymbeline* has been unjustly undervalued because its central character is a woman. Though the play is named after an ancient king of Britain, the plot really centers on his daughter, Innogen. Shakespeare's canon contains many fine female characters, of course, but Innogen may well be the most challenging and complex. The role is occasionally referred to as "the female Hamlet." However, the male roles in this play have not seemed attractive enough to find champions among actors over the centuries, so the play has long been ignored.

Like *Pericles*, the plot of *Cymbeline* is convoluted. King Cymbeline's virtuous daughter, Innogen, has married Posthumus, but the King disapproves of the marriage and banishes him. Innogen, a character whose virtue is drawn in fairytale proportions, faces a range of equally wicked characters. Her evil stepmother, the Queen, is trying to put her loutish son, Cloten, on the throne. In a subplot that seems right out of *Snow White,* the Queen hopes to murder Innogen by poison, but manages only to send her off into a deathlike coma.

Innogen disguises herself as a man, recalling *As You Like It,* to journey to meet her husband. Her adventures lead her to two young men raised in the wild, who, unbeknownst to her, are her long-lost brothers. One of them kills Cloten when he attempts to rape Innogen. She, meanwhile, has unknowingly taken the Queen's poison. One of her brothers lays out her "corpse" alongside the headless body of Cloten. This leads to the most challenging scene in the play, in which Innogen awakes from her drug-induced coma next to what she thinks is the decapitated body of her husband.

Among many other subplots, there is a bizarre wager, which makes Posthumus believe Innogen is unfaithful. He, like Bertram in *All's Well That End's Well,* is a character who falls from grace and is restored only through heavenly intervention—in this case, the literal appearance of Jupiter. The final scene of the play is a long series of wondrous revelations about the real identities of many characters, the unraveling of torturous plot turns, and the reconciliation of all.

Like *Pericles*, the play is purposely written in the style of a folktale set long ago. Its improbable happenings, so magical in good performances, require skill and taste on the part of actors undertaking the roles. Innogen is an especially intense and challenging role because of the vast range of moods and the lightning speed with which they change. The material from this play is good for advanced actors, because it is the most accomplished of Shakespeare's plays that remains relatively unknown and underexposed.

MONOLOGUE SUGGESTIONS

I.iii.17–38. Innogen: "I would have broke mine eye-strings, cracked them, but"
> *Innogen speaks painfully about her husband's departure, which she wished she could have witnessed.*

I.v.10–31. Queen of Britain: "I wonder, doctor"*
> *The Queen refuses to make an excuse for why she wants a vial of poison.*

II.ii.11–51. Giacomo: "The crickets sing, and man's o'er-labored sense"
> *Having surreptitiously entered the room, Giacomo spies on the sleeping Innogen.*

II.v.1–35. Posthumus: "Is there no way for men to be, but women"
> *Posthumus rants, having just heard "proof" that his wife is not faithful.*

III.ii.1–23. Pisanio: "How? Of adultery? Wherefore write you not"
> *Innogen's servant incredulously reads a letter from Innogen's husband accusing her of adultery and ordering her execution.*

III.ii.27–68. Innogen: "O! Learn'd indeed were that astronomer"
> *In high spirits, Innogen hears from her exiled husband that he will be returning.*

III.vi.1–27. Innogen: "I see a man's life is a tedious one"
> *Lost in the woods, Innogen talks herself into enough bravery to enter a cave.*

IV.ii.293–334. Innogen: "Yes, sir, to Milford Haven. Which is the way?"
> *Awakening from a drug-induced coma, Innogen finds the beheaded body, which she wrongly thinks belongs to her husband.*

INTIMATE SCENE SUGGESTIONS

I.iv. *Giacomo bets the naive Posthumus that he can seduce Innogen, Posthumus' wife.*

I.vi. *When his attempt to seduce Innogen fails, Giacomo claims that he was just testing her virtue, but immediately creates another crafty plan of attack.*

II.iii. *With even less style than Giacomo, Cloten propositions Innogen.*

II.iv. *Despite the fact that he was unsuccessful, Giacomo persuades Posthumus that he has seduced his wife, by presenting false but convincing evidence.*

III.iv. *Pisanio reveals that he has been sent by his master, Posthumus, to kill Innogen for her supposed unfaithfulness.*

The Winter's Tale (c. 1610)

Shakespeare adapted Robert Greene's popular prose romance, *Pandosto; or The Triumph of Time*, into his play *The Winter's Tale*. The play begins with a king, Leontes, and his irrational belief that his wife, Hermione, has been unfaithful to him with his best friend, Polixenes (also a king), for which he imprisons and publicly humiliates her in a show trial. She is so grief-stricken that she faints and is soon announced to be dead. Because he believes his newborn child, a daughter, to be a bastard, Leontes rejects her and sends her to be abandoned in the wild.

Like *Pericles*, the play then skips forward in time some sixteen years, via a chorus character named Time. The daughter, Perdita, who was saved by a friendly shepherd, has now grown to most-beautiful-maiden-in-the-village status. She falls in love with Florizel, none other than the son of Polixenes. Polixenes objects to the marriage of his son to a lowly shepherdess, so Florizel and Perdita flee to the court of Leontes. That sad king has realized his error and has spent the last sixteen years in grief, spurred on by reminders from his wife's chief lady-in-waiting, Paulina. In the final act, Leontes is reunited with his daughter, and Perdita's match to Florizel is salvaged. To celebrate, Paulina shows them a miraculous representation of the good queen, Hermione. In what may seem the most improbable of all scenes on the page, and one of the most affecting in the theater, the statue is revealed to be the living Queen, who had been hidden for sixteen years. In performance, the statue coming to life never fails to get audible gasps of surprise and delight.

This play shares with the other romances the difficulty of very complex and varied verse, an extremely convoluted plot, and characters, like Leontes, with unexplained motivations for highly charged emotional reactions. The virtues of *The Winter's Tale*, however, redeem any difficulties it presents. It has superior roles for women, whose suffering is taken seriously and portrayed intensely. There are strong roles for many different types of actors, spanning the entire range of ages. The characters who appear in both halves of this play have the same acting challenges as those acting in *Pericles*, having aged by a generation during the intermission. *The Winter's Tale* can be daunting at first, but it is a great favorite of actors for its depth and challenges.

MONOLOGUE SUGGESTIONS

III.ii. Hermione: "Since what I am to say must be but that"
   The unjustly accused Queen delivers her patient speech of defense.

III.ii. Hermione: "Sir, spare your threats"
   Unfazed by her jealous husband's bullying, Hermione defends her honor.

III.ii. Paulina: "What studied torments, tyrant, hast for me?"
   Hermione's faithful lady-in-waiting reduces the proud King to penitence with the news that his wife is dead due to his haughty, jealousy-driven actions. (The news, by the way, is a trick, but one that is not revealed until the closing scene of the play.)

INTIMATE SCENE SUGGESTIONS

I.ii. *Without success, the courtier Camillo tries to reduce the jealousy of King Leontes.*

II.i. *King Leontes accuses his innocent Queen, Hermione, of adultery.*

III.ii. *The lady-in-waiting, Paulina, tells the King his wife is dead, finally piercing the veil of his irrational jealousy.*

III.iii. *A comic pair, a shepherd and his son, find the abandoned baby, Perdita, and decide to take her home.*

IV.ii. *Now a young woman but unaware that she is a princess, Perdita meets and falls in love with the disguised Prince Florizel.*

IV.iii. *The rogue Autolycus pretends to be the victim of a robbery in order to commit a real one.*

PUBLIC SCENE SUGGESTIONS

II.iii. *Paulina brings the King his baby daughter, though he rejects her as a bastard.*

V.iii. *In front of assembled courtiers, Paulina miraculously restores Leontes' wife to him.*

The Tempest (c. 1611)

Until recently, *The Tempest* was considered to be Shakespeare's last play. Like the earlier romances, this play recounts tragic events that happened in an older generation, and the reconciliation that takes place through a boy and a girl from a new generation. In this case, however, only the later events are dramatized. The equivalent of the first half of *Pericles* or *The Winter's Tale* is told in one long (and difficult) expository scene at the beginning of the play.

The central character, Prospero, has been ousted from his rightful place as Duke of Milan in a coup staged by his brother, aided by the King of Naples. Now many years later, Prospero uses his magical arts to draw his enemies to the island of his exile, where he intends to exact his revenge. In the course of the play, his daughter, Miranda, falls in love with Ferdinand, the son of the King of Naples, and Prospero learns to temper his revenge with mercy. By the end, Prospero is restored to his rightful place as Duke. Because Prospero is a magician, *The Tempest* engages magic directly. Spirits and magical beings inhabit the stage alongside mortals in virtually every scene. The most widely admired and touching scene in the play is a simple one in which Prospero releases his spirit servant, Ariel, to a well-earned freedom.

The play is a theatrical tour-de-force, starting with a (magically induced) storm at sea and containing a brilliant wedding masque. These visually based scenes may not read well, but they are extremely effective in the theater. The mythic quality of the romances is again apparent, along with characters who are more emotionally than logically motivated. The plot, by contrast, is simpler and more straightforward than those of the other romances, which may account for this play's greater popularity and familiarity.

MONOLOGUE SUGGESTIONS

I.ii.1–13. Miranda: "If by your art, my dearest father, you have"
   Prospero's daughter pleads with him to have pity on his victims.
I.ii.324–327, 334–347. Caliban: "As wicked dew as e'er my mother brush'd"
   The wild native, Caliban, challenges Prospero's right to rule the island.

II.ii.18–38. Trinculo: "Here's neither bush nor shrub to bear off any weather"
   In a little comic masterpiece, Trinculo seeks cover on the beach from a storm.
III.iii.53–82. Ariel: "You are three men of sin, whom destiny"
   Godlike, the spirit, Ariel, reveals the sins of the three accused men.
IV.i.148–163. Prospero: "Our revels now are ended."
   In a widely quoted but rarely performed speech, Prospero muses on the power (and limitations) of theater as an art.
V.i.33–57. Prospero: "Ye elves of hills, brooks, standing lakes, and groves"
   The great magician's final conjuring before he gives up his art forever.

INTIMATE SCENE SUGGESTIONS
I.ii. *The magician, Prospero, calls his spirit-servant, Ariel, to congratulate him for a job well done, but also to give him another job before giving him his freedom.*
I.ii. *The first in a pair of scenes in which Prospero's daughter, Miranda, meets the first man she has ever seen, Ferdinand, and falls in love with him.*
II.i. *Antonio, the usurping Duke of Milan, plots with the King of Naples' younger brother, Sebastian, to kill the sleeping King.*
II.ii. *In a comic subplot, Trinculo and Stephano, a pair of drunken clowns, meet the monstrous Caliban and form a conspiracy to overthrow Prospero.*
III.i. *The second Ferdinand–Miranda scene.*

Two Noble Kinsmen (c. 1613) (with John Fletcher)
Unlike most authors of the time, Shakespeare usually wrote his plays without collaborators. Near the end of his career, however, this pattern began to give way, and he wrote several plays that seem to have been at least partly authored by others. His partner for many of them was John Fletcher, the man who would become his replacement as chief dramatist for the King's Men on his retirement. Fletcher had a hand in *All Is True (Henry VIII)*, and perhaps *Pericles* as well.

   Two Noble Kinsmen was entered in contemporary records as having been written jointly by Fletcher and Shakespeare, a statement most scholars now accept as true. It even seems likely that the controlling hand in this project was Fletcher's, as this is the most likely explanation for its absence from the *First Folio*.

Two Noble Kinsmen diverges in some ways from the other romances, but it also has interesting similarities. For example, this play does not have the prominent plot of an older, disenchanted generation finding renewal through a younger one, nor the motif of lost children. It does have a decidedly old-fashioned style (being based on Chaucer), and it invokes gods directly in ways reminiscent of Pericles and Cymbeline. It seems likely that these qualities derive from Shakespeare, though the general plot outline may not.

The story presents two cousins who, like the two gentlemen of Verona, must choose between love and friendship. These best friends, Palamon and Arcite, both find themselves attracted to Emilia and become sworn enemies in rivalry over her. In the end, they agree to fight a duel. The winner will marry Emilia, and the loser will be executed. Arcite wins but is fatally injured in a freak accident just after the duel and generously gives way to Palamon as his dying act. The play has a subplot involving the jailer's daughter, who is desperately in love with Palamon and goes mad from his disinterest.

Two Noble Kinsmen is little known except by specialists, but in recent productions, it has proven sound, even exciting. There is a good deal of extractable material from the play, especially involving the jailer's daughter. (It ought to be noted, in fairness, that most of her speeches are usually assigned to Fletcher's hand rather than Shakespeare's, but they are good material, whoever wrote them.)

MONOLOGUE SUGGESTIONS
I.i.39–55. First Queen: "We are three queens whose sovereigns fell before"
> A queen pleads with Theseus to take revenge against Creon for his mistreatment of her husband's corpse.

I.iii.49–82. Emilia: "I was acquainted"*
> Emilia speaks of a lost playmate and the simplicity of a former time.

II.ii.229–264. Palamon: "Why is he sent for?"
> Hearing of his friend's banishment, Palamon thinks it better than his imprisonment.

II.iii.1–24. Arcite: "Banished the kingdom? 'Tis a benefit"
> In the twin speech to Palamon's, Arcite thinks Palamon's imprisonment better than his banishment.

II.iv. 1–33. Jailer's Daughter: "Why should I love this gentleman?"
The young daughter of the Jailer speaks of her love for one of the prisoners.

II.vi. 1–39. Jailer's Daughter: "Let all the Dukes and devils roar"
Having freed Palamon from prison, and herself from her father, the Jailer's Daughter begins to have her doubts.

III.ii. 1–38. Jailer's Daughter: "He has mistook the brake I meant, is gone"
The Jailer's Daughter begins to realize that Palamon is not coming to meet her.

III.iv. 1–26. Jailer's Daughter: "I am very cold, and all the stars are out too"
Lost and alone, the Jailer's Daughter goes slowly mad.

IV.ii. 1–54. Emilia: "Yet I may bind those wounds up that must open"
Emilia is unable to decide between her suitors.

V.vi. 48–85. Pirithous: "List, then, your cousin"
A messenger tells of Arcite's death and Palamon's reprieve.

INTIMATE SCENE SUGGESTIONS
I.ii; II.ii; III.i; III.iii; III.vi. *In a series of free-standing scenes, the love-hate relationship of Palamon and Arcite is developed.*

Tragicomedies by Shakespeare's Contemporaries

As we have seen, the English dramatists eagerly experimented with new styles and forms in order to entice audiences into the theaters, and only the most classically minded maintained the separation of comedy and tragedy. In fact, almost all the dramatists noted in this book blended comic and tragic elements in one play or another, from early works, such as Greene's *James IV* and Marlowe's *Jew of Malta*, to later satirical plays, such as Marston's *Malcontent* and Shakespeare's *Measure for Measure*.

However, the genre of tragicomedy is most consistently associated with Francis Beaumont and John Fletcher. Their form of tragicomedy involves lyric diction, a strong line of action bringing the characters close to desperate, tragic acts, and then a fortunate conclusion, in which hidden information is revealed to solve the crisis.

The combination of tragedy's inevitable progression of events and comedy's happy ending proved popular with audiences for centuries.

Other dramatists seized on this attractive mixture and developed it in their own ways. Many interesting works could be listed here, but we include a play jointly composed by Dekker, Ford, and Rowley that sets up the comic formula of intrigue and complication and directs it into the sobering conclusions of domestic tragedy.

John Fletcher (1579–1625) and Francis Beaumont (c. 1584–1616)

John Fletcher's and Francis Beaumont's names are inextricably linked, even though they worked together for only five years on six or seven plays, because their collected works were printed under both names in folio in 1647. In fact, several plays in the volume were by Fletcher alone, one was by Beaumont alone, and several others were Fletcher's collaborations with other playwrights. One of the plays in the volume, *Two Noble Kinsmen,* is now recognized as a play written collaboratively by Fletcher and Shakespeare. Fletcher was Shakespeare's collaborator on *All Is True (Henry VIII)* as well.

Fletcher's career overlapped Shakespeare's, but he was Shakespeare's successor in the most literal of ways: as mentioned earlier, upon Shakespeare's retirement, Fletcher became the chief dramatist for the King's Men until his sudden death from plague in 1625. Not surprisingly, his work bears a greater resemblance to Shakespeare's than any other author included here. In the popular romantic comedy, *Philaster,* Beaumont and Fletcher develop the love triangle between lord, lady, and girl-disguised-as-lord's-page that Shakespeare used in *Twelfth Night* and *Two Gentlemen of Verona.* The ensuing gender confusion brings the Princess, Arethusa, and the heir apparent, Philaster, to the brink of tragedy before the true identity of the page, Bellario, is revealed in the last scene. In another popular tragicomedy, *A King and No King,* a potentially incestuous relationship between King Arbaces and his presumed sister, Panthea, is averted when his true parentage is revealed. The subplot about the braggart captain, Bessus, resembles the Parolles subplot in *All's Well That Ends Well.* (Selections from Beaumont and Fletcher's *The Maid's Tragedy* are listed in Chapter 2.)

Philaster (c. 1609)
MONOLOGUE SUGGESTIONS

III.ii. Philaster: "Now you may take that little right I have"
  Philaster bitterly parts from Arethusa, who he believes has betrayed him with his page.
V.v. Bellario/Euphrasia: "My father oft would speak"
  Euphrasia explains why she assumed a boy's disguise to be near Philaster.

SCENE SUGGESTIONS

I.ii. *The princess Arethusa reveals her love to Philaster.*
II.i. *Philaster sends his page, Bellario, to attend Arethusa, but Bellario is reluctant to leave him.*
II.ii. *The lustful Spanish prince, Pharamond, seduces Megra, a lady attending his betrothed.*
III.i. *Philaster, having heard rumors that Arethusa loves his page, Bellario, questions the "boy."*
III.ii. *Philaster suspects the worst when he finds Arethusa in tears at her father's demand that she give up Bellario.*

A King and No King (1611)
MONOLOGUE SUGGESTIONS

III.ii. Bessus: "They talk of fame" and "Certainly my safest way"
  The braggart captain, Bessus, describes how his cowardice has kept him alive over the years.
IV.ii. Tigranes: "Fool that I am, I have undone myself"
  Tigranes wrestles with his old love for Spaconia and his new admiration for Panthea.
IV.ii. Spaconia: "Nay, never hide yourself, for were you hid"
  Spaconia accuses Tigranes of inconstancy.

SCENE SUGGESTIONS

I.i. *Captain Mardonius banters with the cowardly braggart captain, Bessus, about his conduct in the recent wars.*
I.ii. *Spaconia begs her beloved Tigranes not to forget her while he is a prisoner in the Spanish court.*
II.i. *Spaconia appeals to Panthea, the Iberian princess, not to favor Tigranes, whom she has been advised to marry.*
III.ii. *Bessus gives up his sword to Bacurius rather than fight him.*

III.iii. *King Arbaces reveals his passion for his "sister," Panthea, to his advisor, Mardonius.*

III.iii. *King Arbaces employs the rogue Bessus to procure his sister for him, but then rejects him.*

IV.iv. *Arbaces and Panthea admit their mutual attraction but try to avoid further sin.*

Thomas Dekker (c. 1572–1632), William Rowley (c. 1585–1626), and John Ford (1586–after 1639)

Thomas Dekker is best known for his exuberant citizen comedies, and his career is discussed at length in chapter 1. However, he collaborated with many of his contemporaries on all kinds of plays. In 1621, he collaborated with William Rowley, a regular partner with Thomas Middleton, and the young tragedian, John Ford, on *The Witch of Edmonton*. (Other works by Ford and Rowley are described in chapter 2.)

The Witch of Edmonton combines comic and tragic strands in interesting ways. The title character is Old Mother Sawyer, a country woman who decides she might as well become a witch, since everyone already thinks she is one. Her interactions with the Devil and with Cuddy Banks, a foolish local fellow who seeks magical assistance in his love affairs, are written in a forthright comic tone (presumably by Dekker). The main plot, however, is a domestic tragedy in which Frank, who has secretly married the pregnant Winifred, goes ahead with his planned marriage to Susan and then brings about her death. The sexual intrigue customary to revenge tragedies set at court takes on a shocking quality when juxtaposed with the homely village setting and its comic rural types.

The Witch of Edmonton (1621)

SCENE SUGGESTIONS

I.i. *Frank bids farewell to the pregnant Winifred, whom he has just secretly married.*

II.i. *Old Mother Sawyer deals with the Devil, who appears as a black dog (a speaking character played by a human).*

II.i. *The fool, Cuddy Banks, consults Mother Sawyer for help through witchcraft.*

II.ii. *On the morning before their wedding, Susan questions Frank about his misgivings.*

The Golden Age of Spanish Drama

While the great age of English drama flourished on the stages of London, an equally vital theatrical period held sway in Spain. This was the age of Spain's great achievements in naval exploration and its conquest of the New World. With riches pouring in from Mexico and South America, the period from 1580 to 1680 was literally as well as figuratively the "Siglo del Oro," or Golden Age. Philip II, Philip III, and especially Philip IV were lavish patrons of the arts and attracted artists from all over Europe to the newly established court at Madrid. Theater flourished in Madrid and in most of the sizable cities. As in London, writers eagerly experimented with dramatic forms to supply the ravenous demand of audiences in the new professional theaters.

Spanish drama is in many ways similar to that of its Jacobean counterpart in England. More emphasis is placed on violent action and fast-moving, ironic plots than on individual characters. The Spanish dramatists wrote plays in three acts. Like their English counterparts, they wrote primarily for an open stage with little scenic decoration, and scenes flowed from one to the next with little change of decor. The greatest difference is that actresses played women's roles in Spain, though women would not act on English stages until the Restoration. There are many reasons for all actors to take a closer look at Spanish drama, but for actresses especially, there are rich opportunities and a wealth of passionate, opinionated, and challenging characters from which to choose.

Translations and Editions

Of crucial importance in playing Spanish drama is finding good translations. One rendering can be vastly different from another, and it is useful to compare more than one translation (against the Spanish original, if possible) before deciding on your performance text. Keep in mind that many translations are made for readers, not actors, and that a very scholarly edition might not be particularly graceful when spoken out loud.

The Spanish dramatists wrote in verse lines of eight syllables, with no particular stress pattern. The lines were organized into stanzas of four to ten lines, which used various different types of rhyme schemes. The Spanish originals are quick and fluent and shift rapidly in tone and rhythm. You can find English translations like those of Gwynne Edwards, which maintain the eight-syllable lines; or those like Roy Campbell's versions, which use iambic pentameter, like the Elizabethan and Jacobean playwrights; or even prose translations.

Fortunately, there has been a revival of interest in Golden Age plays in the English-speaking theater since 1980, and several good new translations have been made specifically for production use, notably those of Adrian Mitchell. Publishers Aris and Phillips have recently begun to produce a series of Golden Age plays with parallel translations, notes, and introductions. You might also make your own translation, since many scripts by these prolific dramatists have not yet been adapted into English.

Lope Felix de Vega Carpio (1562–1635)

Occupying the same kind of lofty position in Spanish-speaking countries that Shakespeare holds for the English-speaking world,

Lope de Vega is a truly astonishing figure. He bragged that he had written 1500 plays, which may be an exaggeration, but 500 extant plays back up his claim as the most prolific playwright in history.

His life is as incredible as one of his dramas. He was educated by Jesuits in his native Madrid, where he was born to a working-class family. As a young man, he sailed with one of Spain's great exploratory fleets to the Azores. Upon his return to Spain, he was banished from Madrid, but he secretly returned, kidnapping and marrying a young noblewoman. To escape the authorities, he sailed with the Spanish Armada to its historic encounter with the English fleet in 1588. After returning to Spain, he remarried, but outraged the public by living with a series of mistresses and fathering at least sixteen children. Unlikely though it may seem, Lope then became a priest and served as judge and censor for the Inquisition, while simultaneously serving as secretary for the Duke of Sessa.

In 1620, he became the director of Philip III's Court Theater, a post he held until his death fifteen years later. His later life was turbulent and full of loss. In reaction, the playwright gradually withdrew into religious seclusion and poverty. Through it all he kept writing with his customary speed, sometimes penning an entire play in a single day. His death became a cause for national mourning.

Lope de Vega's prodigious output included plays in every genre, from histories to religious plays to tragedies, but most have the satisfying endings we associate with comedies. Alongside the "capa y espada," or cape-and-sword adventures, Lope wrote a number of compelling dramas about peasant honor in the face of aristocratic oppression, such as *Fuenteovejuna* and *Peribañez*. He also developed popular comic formulas around female character types that Spanish dramatists repeated for many years, including the "mujer esquivel," or disdainful woman, plot, and the "bandolera," or female bandit, plot. Lope wrote about scenes and people from real life, eschewing the metaphysics and magic of Calderón and Tirso, yet all of the plays employ his fluid, witty verse.

Scripts for Further Consideration
Fuenteovejuna (The Sheep Well)
El perro del hortelano (The Dog in the Manger)
El castigo sin venganza (Punishment without Revenge)

Peribáñez y el Comendador de Ocaña (*Peribáñez and the Commander of Ocaña*)
El mejor alcalde, el rey (*No Greater Judge Than the King*)
El caballero de Olmedo (*The Knight of Olmedo*)

Tirso de Molina (c. 1584–1648)

Tirso de Molina is the pen name of Fray Gabriel Téllez, a monk, who is widely thought to have been the illegitimate son of the Duke of Osuna. His life, as befitting his calling, was much calmer than either of the other two Spanish playwrights chronicled here. Perhaps the most controversial event in his life was when he was ordered, on pain of excommunication, to stop writing secular plays. He complied, though his work on sacred themes continued unabated. Compared to Lope de Vega's output, Tirso's surviving total of eighty-six plays seems paltry, though he may have written up to four hundred. In comparison to English playwrights, however, this is still a staggering number.

Tirso was the greatest of the "Lopistas," or followers of Lope de Vega, and he followed Lope's successful formulas for intrigue and romantic comedy. Tirso, however, takes a more explicitly political view of his subjects than did Lope (a tendency that may have caused his censorship). He wrote histories and saints' plays as well as secular comedy, and his most famous play, *El burlador de Sevilla* (*The Trickster of Seville*), contains an underpinning of serious religious thought below the sexual antics and comic by-play. This influential work is the first Don Juan play, in which Tirso paints his seductive hero as a dashing rebel against conformity and complacency despite his ultimate damnation. Tirso is famous for his keen intellect, and many of his dazzling heroines show equally acute intelligence as they run circles around the men who try to contain them.

Scripts for Further Consideration

El burlador de Sevilla (*The Trickster of Seville*)
La prudencia en la mujer (*Prudence in Women*)
La gallega Mari-Hernández (*Mari-Hernández from Galicia*)
El condenado por desconfiado (*Damned for Despair*)
Don Gil de las calzas verdes (*Don Gil of the Green Breeches*)

Pedro Calderón de la Barca (1600–1681)

Like his countryman, Lope de Vega, Calderón was educated by Jesuits. His early years involved study of law and theology, travel, and military service. Calderón fought a number of duels, killing his opponent in at least one of them. Despite this stain, he rose quickly to fame. Some of his earliest plays brought him to the attention of the court, where Phillip IV offered him patronage and support.

In his forties, Calderón was deeply affected by both personal crisis and the decline of Spain's national fortunes. His plays became more intensely spiritual and religious, until he retired from the stage altogether to become a priest (a calling he took a great deal more seriously than Lope had) in 1651.

Certainly his most widely admired play in the English-speaking world is *La vida es sueño* (*Life Is a Dream*), which tells the story of a prince, Segismundo, who has been imprisoned since birth to prevent his fulfilling a prophecy that he would become a tyrant. His potentially tragic tale becomes a morally uplifting lesson when he overcomes his brutality and discovers his humanity. The last speech of the second act by Segismundo ("I must control this savagery" in Gwynne Edwards' translation) is one of the most famous speeches in all of Spanish drama, on a par with "To be or not to be." Like *Hamlet*, *La vida es sueño* explores the profound mysteries of art and its attempt to express the ineffable. Indeed, much of Calderón's drama is deeply metaphysical and thoughtful about man's place in the universe, consciously using symbol and artifice to draw attention to the limitations of art. However, his plays are also exciting, suspenseful, and absolutely stageworthy.

Scripts for Further Consideration
La vida es sueño (*Life Is a Dream*)
El médico de su honra (*The Surgeon of Honor*)
El alcalde de Zalamea (*The Mayor of Zalamea*)
El pintor de su dishonra (*The Painter of His Shame*)
El príncipe constante (*The Constant Prince*)
El mágico prodigioso (*The Wonder-Working Magician*)

6 Sonnets and Other Poems

In 1609, as Shakespeare was approaching the end of his writing career, a strange little quarto containing 154 of his sonnets and a longer poem, called "A Lover's Complaint," appeared. Most scholars presume these poems were written as much as a decade earlier, and that they were published in this edition without Shakespeare's cooperation. We know from a reference by Francis Meres, dating from 1598, that Shakespeare had sonnets circulating in manuscript form in literary circles. What we do not know for sure is if the 1609 sonnets are the same as those mentioned by Meres, or why a book of sonnets came about at this point in Shakespeare's career.

There is circumstantial, but still sound, evidence to suggest that the book was immediately taken out of circulation, possibly because Shakespeare himself objected to its publication. The best scholarly speculation is that a publisher got hold of a set of sonnets Shakespeare had written early in his career and published them because he could capitalize on the fame Shakespeare had earned in the intervening years. Shakespeare, according to this theory, immediately used his powerful connections to suppress the book because the sonnets in it were not intended for the general public. Why the authorities might have cooperated is less clear, unless some high ranking person was embarrassed by, or objected to, the content.

This is just the beginning of the mysteries surrounding the sonnets. They tell a fascinating story, but whether it is fictional or autobiographical is a matter of ongoing debate. It is not known if the order in which they are printed is derived from the order in which they were written, or from a narrative arrangement, or if it is a more accidental or arbitrary arrangement. There is a discernible story to the sonnets about an impassioned relationship with a young man that sours when the young man has an affair with the poet's mistress. This story seems to many to be autobiographical, and much scholarly energy has gone into trying to identify the participants, but no direct evidence has ever emerged for any of the possible candidates.

The first 126 sonnets are addressed to a young man. They begin with a series of 17, which urge him to marry and procreate to ensure a form of immortality through his descendants. With number 18, however, they veer off in another direction and never return to this theme again.

With Sonnet 18, the sequence begins to urge another kind of immortality. The poet begins to directly express his devotion and love for the young man and promises him immortality through the agency of poetry. The sonnets continue with a series that speaks of the young man seducing the poet's mistress, leaving him feeling doubly betrayed (Sonnets 40–52), another on the fear of losing the patronage from the young man to a rival poet (Sonnets 78–86), and a group that seems to glancingly refer to an artistic scandal (Sonnets 109–112).

At Sonnet 127 begins a series of poems written about, and to, a mistress with black hair and eyes. This so-called "dark lady" seems to be the same mistress mentioned in the earlier series addressed to the young man.

The sonnets are exceedingly personal, wildly emotional, sensual, and sometimes pointedly sexual. They are witty and literary and at the same time honest and original. In a phrase, they are superb acting material. What follows are some suggestions of favorite sonnets for actors.

Sonnets

18: Shall I compare thee to a summer's day
20: A woman's face with nature's own hand painted
23: As an imperfect actor on the stage
29: When in disgrace with fortune and men's eyes
33: Full many a glorious morning have I seen
44: If the dull substance of my flesh were thought
55: Not marble nor the guilded monuments
57: Being your slave, what should I do but tend
71: No longer mourn for me when I am dead
87: Farewell, thou art too dear for my possessing
94: They that have power to hurt but will do none
116: Let me not to the marriage of true minds
121: 'Tis better to be vile than vile esteemed
129: Th' expense of spirit in a waste of shame
130: My mistress' eyes are nothing like the sun
138: When my love swears she is made of truth
144: Two loves I have, of comfort and despair
147: My love is like a fever, longing still

"A Lover's Complaint"

At the end of the 1609 volume that includes the sonnets, there appears a 329-line poem called "A Lover's Complaint." This work is very uneven, with some superb passages and some rather adolescent ones. It might well have been written by Shakespeare early in his career, as it seems to be closely patterned after a poem called *The Complaint of Rosamund*, which was published in 1592. This is the same year in which we have our first positive reference to Shakespeare living in London.

The poem is the lament of a woman who has been seduced and abandoned, though, as Robert Giroux points out, the last eight lines of the poem shift tone in a rather lamely comic way toward the woman's hope that it will happen again. The poem may be intended to end as a joke rather than in despair.

Because the poem is specifically intended to be read rather than heard, it is less suited than the sonnets to live performance. Of the longer poems, this one has the least extractable material, though lines 288–289, along with the section leading up to them, have often been cited as superior.

Venus and Adonis

Though published long before the Sonnets and "A Lover's Complaint," *Venus and Adonis* was, most presume, written after them. It shows the marks of an accomplished poet.

Unlike the plays, which were kept out of print if at all possible, and the Sonnets, which were designed for a select readership, Shakespeare's two long narrative poems were a bid for literary fame. *Venus and Adonis* was published in 1593, and it accomplished its purpose. The poem became the most published and quoted of all Shakespeare's works in his lifetime. It was considered a piece of "serious" literature at a time when plays were considered as frivolous as we would now consider television scripts.

This poem is not a dramatic work. It is of a very different type. It is a long narrative on a mythological subject. Like the Italian poetry it imitates, it tends toward the erotic. In Shakespeare's time, and most ages between his and ours, the poem was seen as a bit too racy for truly sophisticated tastes, which was part of its appeal. In almost all poems of this type, the eroticism arises from one character ardently pursuing a reluctant lover. In Shakespeare's case, the wit in the poem comes from the reversal of the usual genders of the pursuer and the pursued. Venus is the aggressor here, Adonis the reluctant youth.

Though not intended for performance, the piece is certainly capable of holding the stage.[1] It contains some very imaginative sections. Because the poem is told primarily from Venus' viewpoint, and she is acting atypically as a female aggressor, there are some very powerful extractable sections for women that allow them the kind of presence conventionally associated with male characters.

MONOLOGUE SUGGESTION
Lines 85–174. "O, pity," gan she cry, "flint hearted boy.
　　　　　'Tis but a kiss I beg, why art thou coy?"
Venus' assertion of her suitability to Adonis.

The Rape of Lucrece

Shakespeare's notable contemporary, Gabriel Harvey, wrote, "The younger sort takes much delight in Shakespeare's *Venus and Adonis*, but his *Lucrece*, and his tragedy of *Hamlet, Prince of Denmark*, have it in them to please the wiser sort."

This generous piece of criticism certainly reflects the intent of *The Rape of Lucrece*, if not the current prevailing judgment. In *Lucrece*, Shakespeare was taking on a larger, more difficult task than he had in *Venus and Adonis*. He was writing a more specifically tragic piece, in which sexual obsession has political, as well as personal, consequences. In many ways, modern readers are apt to find this poem generally more conventional and therefore less interesting. The subject of the poem is the rape of a courtier's wife by the son of the Roman king, Tarquin, an act that led Lucius Junius Brutus to spearhead the revolt that evicted the kings from Rome and instituted the Roman Republic.

The poem is, like *Venus*, a nondramatic work but contains extractable sections that actors occasionally use, especially for auditions. The characters are more conventional, but the mood-setting sections of the piece are very powerful. Tarquin's approach to the bed chamber has the same haunting power as Macbeth's progress toward the room in which he will murder the sleeping Duncan. The tragic fascination of a character who knows that he is sealing his fate, but cannot help himself, is present in this poem long before the great tragedies were written.

For original pieces of great intensity, *Lucrece* can be a useful source. The poem employs the conventions of courtly ritual and the rhetoric of chivalry, while ruthlessly exposing the misogynistic underpinnings of these traditions, making it a good choice for demonstrating a feminist perspective.

MONOLOGUE SUGGESTIONS
Lines 190–245. "Fair torch, burn out thy light, and lend it not
                    To darken her whose light excelleth thine."
    Tarquin's thoughts as he approaches the room.
764–1036. "O comfort-killing night, image of hell"
    Lucrece's assumption of blame after the rape.

Note

1. As part of its 1996–1997 season, The Atlanta Shakespeare Company performed the text complete, using some of the conventions of chamber theater. The production was directed by Tony Wright, with an interracial cast of two women. The effect was not realistic, of course, but highly dramatic.

Appendix A: Notes on the Order of Composition of Shakespeare's Plays

o one knows the specific order in which Shakespeare's plays were written. Particularly from the early part of his career, when he was not yet an important figure in the London theater, the records are so sparse as to shed no real light on the question. A great deal of scholarly research has gone into sorting out the very tricky problem of the dates and order of composition of his plays, with limited success.

The following list is a conjectural ordering of the plays; it also lists the theaters for which the various plays were probably written. Few scholarly subjects are as hotly contested as the composition order, and this one will certainly not please all, but it may be of help as a starting place in thinking about the ordering of the plays. All dates and playhouses are guesses, not certainties:

Play	Date	Playhouse
Two Gentlemen of Verona	1589	Theater
King John	1590	Theater
Henry VI, Part 2		
(The First Part of the Contention)	1590	Rose
Henry VI, Part 3		
(Richard, Duke of York)	1591	Rose
The Comedy of Errors	1592	Theater
Henry VI, Part 1	1592	Rose
The Taming of the Shrew	1592	Theater
Titus Andronicus	1592	Rose
Richard III	1593	Theater
Love's Labour's Lost	1593	Theater
Romeo and Juliet	1594	Theater
A Midsummer Night's Dream	1594	Theater

Play	Date	Playhouse
Richard II	1595	Theater
Henry IV, Part 1	1596	Theater
Henry IV, Part 2	1596	Theater
The Merry Wives of Windsor	1597	Curtain
Much Ado About Nothing	1598	Curtain
The Merchant of Venice	1598	Curtain
Henry V	1599	Globe
As You Like It	1600	Globe
Julius Caesar	1600	Globe
Twelfth Night	1600	Globe
Hamlet	1601	Globe
Troilus and Cressida	1602	Globe
Measure for Measure	1603	Globe
Othello	1603	Globe
All's Well That Ends Well	1604	Globe
Timon of Athens	1605	Globe
King Lear	1605	Globe
Macbeth	1606	Globe
Antony and Cleopatra	1606	Globe
Pericles	1607	Globe
Coriolanus	1608	Globe
Cymbeline	1609	Second Blackfriars
The Winter's Tale	1610	Second Blackfriars
The Tempest	1611	Globe
All Is True (Henry VIII)	1613	Globe
Two Noble Kinsmen	1613	Second Globe

Appendix B: About the Selection Guides

"I'm looking for a monologue ..."

As actors, directors, and teachers, we know how challenging and frustrating the search for material can be. Acting students always need a good, new monologue. (One teacher expected her students to have nine monologues ready at any time!) Scene study classes require a steady supply of scenes which are challenging, exciting, and (we all pray) not overly familiar. And of course auditions, especially for graduate schools, often call for contrasting comic and serious, or classical and contemporary, or verse and prose selections.

In this guide, we have tried to identify some of the major styles, plays, and dramatists of the Shakespearean era, both familiar and unfamiliar. What follows now are indexes to the material which categorize early modern selections in more contemporary (and often irreverently pragmatic) terms.

Our indexes are unavoidably subjective. As any good actor knows, any scene can be interpreted in many different ways. There are funny speeches from serious plays. There are darkly comic speeches that seem more appropriate for "dramatic" auditions. There are characters that were once played by young boys that now are usually played by mature women. There are hosts of speeches that are usually delivered by adult men in the theater, but which make ideal classroom exercises for students of both genders and all ages.

To get bogged down in these complications, however, is to give in to the very problem that makes indexes useful in the first place. Students and actors already know how hard it is to find a piece that is just right for the occasion, suitable to the performer, and interpreted in a way at least acceptable to the auditor/instructor. In our experience, what is needed is helpful hints, not more ambiguities.

At the risk, then, of offending some sensibilities, we have created these indexes. In the following pages we describe a few guidelines which governed our choices.

Genre and Tone: Serious and Comic

The previous chapters of this book have discussed various plays according to genre and sub-genre (tragedy, revenge tragedy, etc.). However, actors looking for independent scenes or monologues often sort material into only two broad categories, serious or comic. Accordingly, these indexes use only these two categories.

We have categorized only the selection itself, not the play from which it comes. Therefore, you will find that some "serious" speeches and scenes have been taken from plays described in the Comedies chapter. These selections have the depth and seriousness that make them appropriate for "serious" auditions, even though the overall plays have the structure and tone of comedy. It is to your advantage to know what the tone of the piece is, as well as the traditional genre of the play.

Characters: Age, Gender, and Type

"Am I right for the part?"

Shakespeare and his contemporaries wrote for specific troupes of actors, many of whom specialized in certain popular types of roles. The great clown Will Kempe inspired many clown characters, for instance, whereas many of Marlowe's tragic heroes were written for the particular talents of Edward Alleyn. Actors today will find it helpful to think about the similarities between characters of a given type, and choose their audition material appropriately. For instance, if you hope to be cast as the witty maid Lucetta in Shakespeare's *Two Gentlemen of Verona*, you might select a scene from a similar character type for your audition.

In the neoclassical tradition which Shakespeare and his contemporaries embraced, characters often fell into certain standard "types." Young marriageable characters (often referred to as ingenues and juveniles) appeared abundantly in comedies as young lovers, and as sons and daughters in more serious plays. The young lovers were often contrasted with companions, confidantes, and servants. These secondary, more eccentric roles were given the ambiguous name of "character" parts; in the indexes we use this term only to imply that these parts offer some sort of contrast to the young marriageable types. Similar contrasts define the leading adult characters from their "character part" attendants and supporters. However, a "character" part is sometimes the starring role. For instance, in Shakespeare's *Much Ado About Nothing* the witty, comic parts of Beatrice and Benedick are essentially "character parts," in that they are contrasted with the ingenuous young lovers, Hero and Claudio; yet Beatrice and Benedick are usually the central focus of most modern productions. "Character part" certainly does not mean "minor role"!

Characters in the index are described by a very limited set of descriptors. We have indicated whether the character is usually played in the modern theater by a child, by a young person (by which we mean roughly the traditional age of college students), or by adults (by which we mean anyone older than traditional aged college students) as the only age distinctions. We have then gone on to subdivide those groupings into "character" and "non-character" types.

Finally, we have carefully tried to indicate the gender of the *characters*, which should not be read to mean that we think only actors of the specified gender can play the parts. The issue of gender is remarkably complex, given that female roles were all played by boy actors on English stages in the early modern period. These female characters, furthermore, often assume male disguise, thus creating a complicated layering of performed sexuality. In the contemporary theater, actors increasingly play characters of different genders, but such casting is often intended to be a "statement." Who gets to play which role is a hot issue in the modern theater, and one in which we, frankly, tend to side with those trying to stir up as much change as possible; we simply urge awareness about the play and its context before making such choices.

Some characters, especially chorus figures, really have no gender and have long traditions of being played by both men and women, so we have listed these separately.

Verse and Prose

Some auditions ask actors to demonstrate facility with handling verse, as opposed to simply performing pieces from the early modern repertoire. We have, therefore, noted the dominant mode of scenes and monologues. Occasionally a verse piece will have a very short interlude of prose, or vice versa, but the categories are generally dependable enough to judge the appropriateness of the piece for an audition.

Numbers

In these indexes there are a few occasions where a character or set of characters has more than one selection listed in the earlier portion of the book. In these cases the number of speeches or scenes appears immediately after the character(s) name(s). For example:

Romeo and Juliet   Romeo young m (2)   verse

If a number appears before a play name, as in *2 Henry IV,* then it indicates that this is the play *Henry the Fourth, Part Two.* This indication may, at first, seem confusing to those not familiar with the early modern convention of naming sequels as new "parts." It is just the same as the modern tendency to name movies the same thing over and over again with just a new number behind them. As I write the box office rage is *Scream 2,* which, everyone knows, is a totally new movie, related to, but different from *Scream.*

Final Words

We don't intend our judgment to substitute for your judgment. These indexes were created to help speed the process of finding and exploring material. Each entry here is cross-referenced with the page number of a more detailed and informative discussion earlier in the book. We encourage you to read those discussions carefully and to think about the appropriateness of the piece for you, for the occasions, and for the given set of auditors. We hope these indexes help lead you to a broader familiarity with Shakespearean works and with works of his contemporaries. Keep exploring. While not every piece will work for every actor, we think the number of new and challenging possibilities will be a boon to any search for material.

Appendix C: Selection Guide to Monologues

Serious Monologues for Ungendered Characters

Title	Character	Type	Language	Page
2 Henry IV	Rumor	—	verse	80
Henry V	Chorus (2)	—	verse	82
The Tempest	Ariel	—	verse	103
Troilus and Cressida	Prologue	—	verse	29

Serious Monologues for Female Characters

Title	Character	Type	Language	Page
All's Well That Ends Well	Helena	young w	verse	32
Cymbeline	Innogen (3)	young w	verse	99
Hamlet	Ophelia	young w	verse	50
1 Henry IV	Lady Percy	young w	verse	79
2 Henry IV	Lady Percy	young w	verse	80
1 Henry VI	Joan (4)	young w	verse	83
Measure for Measure	Isabella	young w	verse	31
Othello	Desdemona	young w	verse	53
Richard III	Lady Anne (2)	young w	verse	88
Romeo and Juliet	Juliet	young w	verse	49
The Tempest	Miranda	young w	verse	103
Two Noble Kinsmen	Emilia (2)	young w	verse	104
The Atheist's Tragedy	Castabella	young w	verse	45
Edward II	Isabella	young w	verse	92
2 The Fair Maid of the West	Bess	young w	verse	25
The Maid's Tragedy	Aspatia	young w	verse	46
Perkin Warbeck	Katherine (2)	young w	verse	92
Philaster	Bellario/ Euphrasia	young w	verse	108
The Spanish Tragedy	Bel-Imperia	young w	verse	44
'Tis Pity She's a Whore	Annabella	young w	verse	73
Volpone	Celia	young w	verse	21
Women Beware Women	Isabella	young w	verse	71
Two Noble Kinsmen	Jailer's daughter (3)	young char w	verse	104
A King and No King	Spaconia	young char w	verse	108
All Is True	Katharine	adult w	verse	90
Antony and Cleopatra	Cleopatra (4)	adult w	verse	61
Coriolanus	Volumnia	adult w	prose	63
Coriolanus	Volumnia	adult w	verse	63
Cymbeline	Queen	adult w	verse	99
Hamlet	Gertrude	adult w	verse	50
2 Henry VI	Eleanor (2)	adult w	verse	85
2 Henry VI	Margaret	adult w	verse	85

Title	Character	Type	Language	Page
3 Henry VI	Margaret (2)	adult w	verse	86
Julius Caesar	Portia	adult w	verse	60
Julius Caesar	Calpurnia	adult w	verse	60
King John	Constance (2)	adult w	verse	76
King Lear	Goneril	adult w	verse	55
Macbeth	Lady Macbeth	adult w	verse	54
A Midsummer Night's Dream	Titania	adult w	verse	7
Richard III	Margaret	adult w	verse	88
Titus Andronicus	Tamora	adult w	verse	42
Two Noble Kinsmen	First Queen	adult w	verse	104
The Winter's Tale	Hermione (2)	adult w	verse	101
The Changeling	Beatrice	adult w	mixed	72
The Duchess of Malfi	Duchess (2)	adult w	verse	70
1 The Honest Whore	Bellafront	adult w	verse	23
2 The Honest Whore	Bellafront (2)	adult w	verse	23
The Maid's Tragedy	Evadne	adult w	verse	46
The Revenge of Bussy D'Ambois	Tamyra	adult w	verse	48
The Revenge of Bussy D'Ambois	Countess	adult w	verse	48
The Revenger's Tragedy	Duchess	adult w	verse	45
Sejanus	Agrippina	adult w	verse	66
1 Tamburlaine	Zenocrate	adult w	verse	59
'Tis Pity She's a Whore	Hippolita	adult w	verse	73
The White Devil	Vittoria	adult w	verse	70
Women Beware Women	Bianca (2)	adult w	verse	71
Macbeth	Hecate	adult char w	verse	54
Pericles	Dionyza (2)	adult char w	verse	97
The Winter's Tale	Paulina	adult char w	verse	101
The Atheist's Tragedy	Levidulcia	adult char w	verse	45
The Spanish Tragedy	Isabella (2)	adult char w	verse	44
The Witch	Hecate	adult char w	verse	72

Serious Monologues for Male Characters

Title	Character	Type	Language	Page
1 Henry IV	Prince Hal (2)	young m	verse	79
2 Henry IV	Prince Hal (2)	young m	verse	80
2 Henry VI	Young Clifford	young m	verse	85
King John	Prince Henry	young m	verse	76
King Lear	Edgar	young m	verse	55
Measure for Measure	Claudio	young m	verse	31
Romeo and Juliet	Romeo (2)	young m	verse	49
Troilus and Cressida	Troilus	young m	verse	29
Two Gentlemen of Verona	Proteus	young m	verse	2
Two Noble Kinsmen	Palamon	young m	verse	104
Two Noble Kinsmen	Arcite	young m	verse	104
Two Noble Kinsmen	Pirithous	young m	verse	104
Antonio and Mellida	Antonio (2)	young m	verse	37
The Atheist's Tragedy	Charlemont	young m	verse	45
1 The Honest Whore	Hippolito (2)	young m	verse	23
James IV	King	young m	verse	12
The Maid's Tragedy	Amintor	young m	verse	46
Perkin Warbeck	Warbeck	young m	verse	92
Philaster	Philaster	young m	verse	108
'Tis Pity She's a Whore	Giovanni	young m	verse	73
A Woman Killed with Kindness	Wendoll	young m	verse	68
Women Beware Women	Leantio (2)	young m	verse	71
King John	Bastard	young char m	verse	76
King Lear	Edmund	young char m	verse	55
The Tempest	Ariel	young char	verse	103
The Revenger's Tragedy	Spurio	young char m	verse	45
The Spanish Tragedy	Page	young char/boy	prose	44
Antony and Cleopatra	Antony (2)	adult m	verse	61
Coriolanus	Coriolanus (3)	adult m	verse	63
Hamlet	Hamlet (3)	adult m	verse	50

Title	Character	Type	Language	Page
Hamlet	Horatio	adult m	verse	50
Hamlet	Laertes	adult m	verse	50
Hamlet	Claudius	adult m	verse	50
1 Henry IV	Henry IV	adult m	verse	79
2 Henry IV	Henry IV	adult m	verse	80
Henry V	Henry V (3)	adult m	verse	82
1 Henry VI	Talbot	adult m	verse	83
2 Henry VI	Jack Cade	adult m	prose	85
3 Henry VI	Henry VI	adult m	verse	86
3 Henry VI	Clifford	adult m	verse	86
Julius Caesar	Caesar	adult m	verse	60
Julius Caesar	Brutus	adult m	verse	60
Julius Caesar	Antony (2)	adult m	verse	60
King Lear	Lear	adult m	verse	55
Macbeth	Macbeth (3)	adult m	verse	54
Measure for Measure	Angelo	adult m	verse	31
Othello	Othello (3)	adult m	verse	53
Pericles	Pericles	adult m	verse	97
Richard II	Richard II (4)	adult m	verse	77
Richard II	Bolingbroke	adult m	verse	77
Richard III	Richmond	adult m	verse	88
The Tempest	Prospero (2)	adult m	verse	103
Titus Andronicus	Titus	adult m	verse	42
Antonio and Mellida	Andrugio (2)	adult m	verse	37
The Atheist's Tragedy	D'Amville	adult m	verse	45
The Broken Heart	Bassanes	adult m	verse	74
Catiline	Catiline (3)	adult m	verse	67
Catiline	Cicero	adult m	verse	67
Catiline	Petreius	adult m	verse	67
Doctor Faustus	Faustus	adult m	verse	59
The Duchess of Malfi	Ferdinand (2)	adult m	verse	70
Edward II	Edward II	adult m	verse	92
A King and No King	Tigranes	adult m	verse	108
Perkin Warbeck	Dawbney	adult m	verse	92
The Revenger's Tragedy	Vindice (2)	adult m	verse	45
The Revenge of Bussy D'Ambois	Clermont (4)	adult m	verse	48
Sejanus	Silius	adult m	verse	66
Sejanus	Terentius	adult m	verse	66
The Spanish Tragedy	Hieronimo (3)	adult m	verse	44
1 Tamburlaine	Tamburlaine	adult m	verse	59

Title	Character	Type	Language	Page
2 Tamburlaine	Tamburlaine (2)	adult m	verse	59
The White Devil	Francisco de Medici	adult m	verse	70
The Witch	Sebastian	adult m	verse	72
A Woman Killed with Kindness	Sir Charles	adult m	verse	68
A Woman Killed with Kindness	Frankford	adult m	verse	68
All Is True	Wolsey	adult char m	verse	90
Antony and Cleopatra	Enobarbus	adult char m	verse	61
Cymbeline	Giacomo	adult char m	verse	99
Cymbeline	Pisanio	adult char m	verse	99
Richard II	John of Gaunt	adult char m	verse	77
Hamlet	Ghost	adult char m	verse	50
3 Henry VI	Richard Glouc. (2)	adult char m	verse	86
Julius Caesar	Cassius	adult char m	verse	60
Macbeth	Captain	adult char m	verse	54
Measure for Measure	Duke	adult char m	verse	31
Othello	Iago	adult char m	verse	53
Richard III	Tyrrell	adult char m	verse	88
Timon of Athens	Timon	adult char m	verse	65
Titus Andronicus	Aaron (2)	adult char m	verse	42
The Atheist's Tragedy	Borachio	adult char m	verse	45
The Changeling	De Flores	adult char m	verse	72
The Fawn	Hercules	adult char m	verse	35
James IV	Bishop	adult char m	verse	12
The Malcontent	Malevole (2)	adult char m	verse	36
The Malcontent	Mendoza	adult char m	verse	36
Perkin Warbeck	Bishop of Durham	adult char m	verse	92
The Revenge of Bussy D'Ambois	Aumale	adult char m	verse	48
Sejanus	Sejanus	adult char m	verse	66
Sejanus	Tiberius	adult char m	verse	66
'Tis Pity She's a Whore	Friar	adult char m	verse	73
The White Devil	Flamineo	adult char m	verse	70
A Woman Killed with Kindness	Nicholas	adult char m	verse	68

Comic Monologues for Female Characters

Title	Character	Type	Language	Page
All's Well That Ends Well	Helena (2)	young w	verse	32
As You Like It	Rosalind	young w	prose	15
As You Like It	Rosalind	young w	verse	15
Cymbeline	Innogen	young w	verse	99
Love's Labour's Lost	Princess	young w	verse	6
The Merchant of Venice	Portia	young w	verse	28
Troilus and Cressida	Cressida	young w	verse	29
Twelfth Night	Viola	young w	verse	16
Two Gentlemen of Verona	Julia (2)	young w	verse	2
Campaspe	Campaspe	young w	prose	10
Friar Bacon and Friar Bungay	Margaret (2)	young w	verse	12
Gallathea	Phillida	young w	prose	11
As You Like It	Phebe	young char w	verse	15
A Midsummer Night's Dream	Helena	young char w	verse	7
Two Noble Kinsmen	Jailer's Daughter	young char w	verse	104
The City Madam	Anne	young char w	verse	38
The City Madam	Mary	young char w	verse	38
The Shoemakers' Holiday	Sybil	young char w	prose	23
The Witch	Francisca	young char w	prose	72
2 Henry VI	Margaret	adult w	verse	85
The Merry Wives of Windsor	Mrs. Page	adult w	prose	17
The Comedy of Errors	Adriana	adult char w	verse	4
2 Henry IV	Quickly	adult char w	prose	80
Henry V	Quickly	adult char w	prose	82
Much Ado About Nothing	Beatrice	adult char w	verse	13
Othello	Emilia	adult char w	mixed	53
The Taming of the Shrew	Kate	adult char w	verse	5
Twelfth Night	Olivia	adult char w	verse	16
The Alchemist	Dol Common	adult char w	verse	22

Title	Character	Type	Language	Page
Bartholomew Fair	Ursula	adult char w	prose	22
A Chaste Maid in Cheapside	Maudline	adult char w	verse	25
Epicoene	Mrs. Otter	adult char w	prose	22
The Fawn	Zoya	adult char w	prose	35
The Fawn	Puttotta	adult char w	prose	35
A Mad World, My Masters	Mother	adult char w	verse	25
'Tis Pity She's a Whore	Putana	adult char w	prose	73
Volpone	Lady Politic	adult char w	verse	21

Comic Monologues for Male Characters

Title	Character	Type	Language	Page
Henry V	Boy	child	prose	82
Love's Labour's Lost	King	young m	verse	6
Love's Labour's Lost	Longueville	young m	verse	6
Love's Labour's Lost	Dumaine	young m	verse	6
Troilus and Cressida	Troilus	young m	verse	29
Twelfth Night	Sebastian	young m	verse	16
Two Gentlemen of Verona	Proteus	young m	verse	2
Two Gentlemen of Verona	Valentine	young m	verse	2
Campaspe	Apelles	young m	prose	10
Edward II	Gaveston	young m	verse	92
Endimion	Endimion	young m	prose	10
The Comedy of Errors	Dromio E.	young char m	prose	4
1 Henry IV	Hotspur	young char m	verse	79
King John	Bastard	young char m	verse	76
King Lear	Edmund	young char m	prose	55
Love's Labour's Lost	Biron	young char m	verse	6
Love's Labour's Lost	Biron	young char m	prose	6
A Chaste Maid in Cheapside	Tim	young char m	verse	25
2 The Fair Maid of the West	Clem	young char m	prose	27
Volpone	Mosca	young char m	verse	21
As You Like It	Duke Senior	adult m	verse	15
The Merry Wives of Windsor	Ford	adult m	prose	17
A Midsummer Night's Dream	Oberon (2)	adult m	verse	7
Troilus and Cressida	Hector	adult m	verse	29
Campaspe	Hephestion	adult m	prose	10
The City Madam	Plenty	adult m	verse	38
Every Man in His Humour	Knowell	adult m	verse	21
Epicoene	Truewit (3)	adult m	prose	22
All's Well That Ends Well	Parolles	adult char m	prose	32
As You Like It	Jaques	adult char m	verse	15
1 Henry IV	Falstaff (2)	adult char m	prose	79
2 Henry IV	Falstaff	adult char m	prose	80
Hamlet	Polonius	adult char m	verse	50

Title	Character	Type	Language	Page
Love's Labour's Lost	Don Armado	adult char m	prose	6
Macbeth	Porter	adult char m	prose	54
The Merchant of Venice	Shylock	adult char m	verse	28
Much Ado About Nothing	Benedick (2)	adult char m	prose	13
Richard III	Richard (2)	adult char m	verse	88
The Taming of the Shrew	Petruccio (2)	adult char m	verse	5
The Tempest	Caliban	adult char m	verse	103
The Tempest	Trinculo	adult char m	prose	103
Troilus and Cressida	Thersites	adult char m	prose	29
Two Gentlemen of Verona	Lance	adult char m	prose	2
The Alchemist	Sir Epicure	adult char m	verse	22
Campaspe	Melippus	adult char m	prose	10
A Chaste Maid in Cheapside	Allwit	adult char m	verse	25
A Chaste Maid in Cheapside	Touch-wood Sr.	adult char m	verse	25
The City Madam	Luke (3)	adult char m	verse	38
Epicoene	La Foole	adult char m	prose	22
Every Man Out of his Humour	Carlo Buffone	adult char m	prose	21
Every Man Out of his Humour	Fastidious Brisk	adult char m	prose	21
The Fawn	Hercules	adult char m	prose	35
The Fawn	Nymphadoro	adult char m	prose	35
The Fawn	Zuccone	adult char m	prose	35
Friar Bacon and Friar Bungay	Friar Bacon	adult char m	verse	12
James IV	Ateukin	adult char m	verse	12
A King and No King	Bessus	adult char m	prose	108
A Mad World, My Masters	Penitent Brothel	adult char m	verse	25
The Malcontent	Malevole	adult char m	mixed	36
The Malcontent	Mendoza	adult char m	prose	36
The Shoemakers' Holiday	Simon Eyre	adult char m	prose	23
The Witch	Almachildes	adult char m	mixed	72

Appendix D:
Selection Guide to Scenes

Serious Scenes for Two Female Characters

Title	Character	Type	Language	Page
Othello	Desdemona	young w	verse	53
	Emilia	adult char w		
Romeo and Juliet	Juliet	young w	verse	49
	Nurse	adult char w		
The Broken Heart	Penthea	adult w	verse	74
	Calantha	young w		
The Duchess of Malfi	Duchess	adult w	verse	70
	Cariola	adult char w		
A King and No King	Spaconia	young char w	verse	108
	Panthea	young w		
The Revenger's Tragedy	Castiza	young w	verse	45
	Gratiana	adult char w		
Women Beware Women	Livia	adult char w	verse	71
	Isabella	young w		

Serious Scenes by Shakespeare for One Female and One Male Character

Title	Character	Type	Language	Page
All Is True	Katharine	adult w	verse	90
	Griffith	adult m		
Antony and Cleopatra	Cleopatra	adult w	verse	61
	Antony	adult m		
Antony and Cleopatra	Cleopatra	adult w	prose	61
	Clown	adult char m		
Antony and Cleopatra	Cleopatra	adult w	verse	61
	Antony	adult m		
Coriolanus	Coriolanus	adult m	verse	63
	Volumnia	adult w		
Cymbeline	Giacomo	adult char	verse	99
	Innogen	young w		
Cymbeline	Pisanio	young char	verse	99
	Innogen	young w		
Hamlet	Ophelia	young w	verse	50
	Polonius	adult char m		
Hamlet	Gertrude	adult w	verse	50
	Hamlet	adult m		
Hamlet	Ophelia	young w	verse	50
	Hamlet	adult m		
1 Henry VI	Joan	young w	verse	83
	Dauphin	adult m		
1 Henry VI	Countess	adult char w	verse	83
	Talbot	adult m		
2 Henry VI	Gloucester	adult char m	verse	85
	Duchess	adult w		
2 Henry VI	Margaret	adult w	verse	85
	Suffolk	adult char m		
Julius Caesar	Portia	adult w	verse	60
	Brutus	adult m		
Julius Caesar	Calpurnia	adult w	verse	60
	Caesar	adult m		
King Lear	Goneril	adult w	verse	55
	Albany	adult char m		
King Lear	Lear	adult m	verse	55
	Regan	adult w		
Macbeth	Macbeth} (2)	adult m	verse	54
	Lady Macbeth}	adult w		

Title	Character	Type	Language	Page
Measure for Measure	Isabella	young w	verse	31
	Lucio	adult char m		
Measure for Measure	Isabella	young w	verse	31
	Angelo	adult m		
Measure for Measure	Isabella	young w	verse	31
	Claudio	young m		
Othello	Othello}	adult m	verse	53
	Desdemona} (3)	young w		
Pericles	Dionyza	adult char w	verse	97
	Cleon	adult char m		
Pericles	Pericles	adult m	verse	97
	Marina	young w		
Richard II	Queen	adult w	verse	77
	Richard II	adult m		
Richard III	Richard	adult char m	verse	88
	Elizabeth	adult w		
Richard III	Richard	adult char m	verse	88
	Lady Anne	young w		
Romeo and Juliet	Romeo	young m	verse	49
	Juliet	young w		
Romeo and Juliet	Romeo	young m	verse	49
	Juliet	young w		
Romeo and Juliet	Friar	adult char m	verse	49
	Juliet	young w		
Titus Andronicus	Tamora	adult w	verse	42
	Aaron	adult char m		
Titus Andronicus	Tamora	adult w	verse	42
	Titus	adult m		
The Winter's Tale	Leontes	adult m	verse	101
	Hermione	adult w		
The Winter's Tale	Paulina	adult char w	verse	101
	Leontes	adult m		

Serious Scenes by Other Dramatists for One Female and One Male Character

Title	Character	Type	Language	Page
The Atheist's Tragedy	Charlemont	young m	verse	45
	Castabella	young w		
The Broken Heart	Penthea	adult w	verse	74
	Orgilus	adult m		
The Broken Heart	Penthea	adult w	verse	74
	Ithocles	adult m		
Catiline	Fulvia	adult w	verse	67
	Curius	adult m		
The Changeling	Beatrice} (3)	adult w	verse	72
	De Flores}	adult char m		
The Duchess of Malfi	Duchess	adult w	verse	70
	Antonio	adult m		
The Duchess of Malfi	Duchess	adult w	verse	70
	Bosola	adult char m		
The Duchess of Malfi	Bosola	adult char m	verse	70
	Julia	adult char w		
The Duchess of Malfi	Julia	adult char w	verse	70
	Cardinal	adult char m		
1 The Honest Whore	Hippolito	young m	verse	23
	Bellafront	adult w		
2 The Honest Whore	Bellafront	adult w	verse	23
	Orlando	adult char m		
James IV	Ida	young w	verse	12
	Ateukin	adult char m		
The Jew of Malta	Barabas	adult char m	verse	59
	Abigall	young w		
A King and No King	Tigranes	adult m	verse	108
	Spaconia	young char w		
A King and No King	Arbaces	young m	verse	108
	Panthea	young w		
The Maid's Tragedy	Evadne	adult w	verse	46
	Amintor	young m		
The Maid's Tragedy	Evadne	adult w	verse	46
	Melantius	young m		
The Maid's Tragedy	Evadne	adult w	verse	46
	King	adult m		
The Malcontent	Mendoza	adult char m	verse	36
	Aurelia	young char w		

Title	Character	Type	Language	Page
Perkin Warbeck	Katherine Warbeck	young w young m	verse	92
Philaster	Pharamond Megra	adult char m adult char w	mixed	108
Philaster	Philaster Bellario/Euphrasia	young m young w	verse	108
Philaster	Philaster} (2) Arethusa}	young m young w	verse	108
The Revenger's Tragedy	Vindice Gratiana	adult m adult char w	verse	45
'Tis Pity She's a Whore	Annabella Giovanni	young w young m	verse	73
'Tis Pity She's a Whore	Annabella Soranzo	young w adult m	verse	73
'Tis Pity She's a Whore	Vasquez Putana	adult char m adult char w	prose	73
The White Devil	Isabella Brachiano	adult w adult m	verse	70
The Witch of Edmonton	Frank Winifred	young m young w	verse	109
The Witch of Edmonton	Frank Susan	young m young w	verse	109
A Woman Killed with Kindness	Anne Wendoll	young w young m	verse	68
A Woman Killed with Kindness	Sir Charles Susan	adult m young char w	verse	68
Women Beware Women	Bianca Leantio	adult w young m	verse	71

Serious Scenes by Shakespeare for Two Male Characters

Title	Character	Type	Language	Page
All Is True	Buckingham	adult m	verse	90
	Norfolk	adult m		
All Is True	Wolsey	adult char m	verse	90
	Cromwell	adult m		
Antony and Cleopatra	Antony	adult m	verse	61
	Eros	young m		
Coriolanus	Sicinius	adult m	verse	63
	Brutus	adult m		
Coriolanus	Nicanor	adult char m	prose	63
	Adrian	adult char m		
Coriolanus	Coriolanus	adult m	verse	63
	Aufidius	adult m		
Coriolanus (public)	Coriolanus	adult m	verse	63
	Cominius	adult m		
Cymbeline	Giacomo	adult char m	verse	99
	Posthumus	young m		
Hamlet	Horatio	adult m	verse	50
	Hamlet	adult m		
Hamlet	Hamlet	adult m	verse	50
	Ghost	adult char m		
Hamlet (public)	Hamlet	adult m	verse	50
	Claudius	adult m		
1 Henry IV	Hotspur	young char m	verse	79
	Worcester	adult m		
2 Henry IV	Henry IV	adult m	verse	80
	Prince Hal	young m		
Henry V	Henry V	adult m	prose	82
	Williams	young char m		
1 Henry VI	Talbot	adult m	verse	83
	John Talbot	young m		
2 Henry VI	Jack Cade	adult m	mixed	85
	Iden	adult m		
3 Henry VI	Henry VI	adult m	verse	86
	Richard Gloucester	adult char m		
Julius Caesar	Brutus} (3)	adult m	verse	60
	Cassius}	adult char m		
King John	King John	adult m	verse	76
	Hubert	adult char m		

Title	Character	Type	Language	Page
King John	Arthur	child	verse	76
	Hubert	adult char m		
King John	King John	adult m	verse	76
	Hubert	adult char m		
King Lear	Edmund} (2)	young char m	prose	55
	Gloucester}	adult char m		
King Lear	Edgar	young m	verse	55
	Gloucester	adult char m		
Macbeth	Macduff	adult m	verse	54
	Malcolm	young m		
Measure for Measure	Duke	adult char m	prose	31
	Provost	adult char m		
Othello	Iago	adult char m	prose	53
	Cassio	adult m		
Othello	Iago} (2)	adult char m	prose	53
	Roderigo}	young char m		
Othello	Iago	adult char m	verse	53
	Othello	adult m		
Richard II	Bolingbroke	adult m	verse	77
	John of Gaunt	adult char m		
Richard II	York	adult m	verse	77
	Bolingbroke	adult m		
Richard III	Richard	adult char m	verse	88
	Buckingham	adult m		
Richard III	Richard	adult char m	verse	88
	Buckingham	adult m		
Romeo and Juliet	Romeo} (2)	young m	verse	49
	Friar}	adult char m		
The Tempest	Antonio	adult char m	verse	103
	Sebastian	adult char m		
Timon of Athens	Timon	adult char m	verse	65
	Apemantus	adult char m		
Timon of Athens	Timon} (2)	adult char m	verse	65
	Flavius}	adult char m		
Two Gentlemen of Verona	Duke	adult m	verse	2
	Valentine	young m		
Two Noble Kinsmen	Palamon} (5)	young m	verse	104
	Arcite}	young m		
The Winter's Tale	Leontes	adult m	verse	101
	Camillo	adult char m		

Serious Scenes by Other Dramatists for Two Male Characters

Title	Character	Type	Language	Page
The Atheist's Tragedy	D'Amville	adult m	verse	45
	Borachio	adult char m		
Doctor Faustus	Faustus} (2)	adult m	verse	59
	Mephistophilis	adult char m		
The Duchess of Malfi	Ferdinand	adult m	verse	70
	Cardinal	adult char m		
Edward II	Edward II	adult m	verse	92
	Gaveston	young m		
Edward II	Edward II	adult m	verse	92
	Lightborn	adult m		
James IV	King} (2)	young m	verse	12
	Ateukin	adult char m		
The Jew of Malta	Barabas	adult char m	verse	59
	Ithimore	adult char m		
A King and No King	Arbaces	young m	verse	108
	Mardonius	adult m		
The Maid's Tragedy	Amintor	young m	verse	46
	Melantius	young m		
The Revenger's Tragedy	Lussurioso	adult char m	verse	45
	Vindice	adult m		
Sejanus	Sejanus	adult char m	verse	66
	Eudemus	adult m		
A Woman Killed with Kindness	Frankford	adult m	verse	68
	Nicholas	adult char m		

Serious Scenes for Three Characters

Title	Character	Type	Language	Page
Hamlet (public)	Hamlet	adult m	verse	50
	Claudius	adult m		
Measure for Measure	Isabella	young w	verse	31
	Lucio	adult char m		
	Angelo	adult m		
Troilus and Cressida	Ulysses	adult m	verse	29
	Agamemnon	adult m		
	Nestor	adult char m		
Friar Bacon and	Lacy	young m	verse	12
Friar Bungay	Margaret	young w		
	Edward	young m		
The Revenge of	Charlotte	adult w	verse	48
Bussy D'Ambois	Clermont	adult m		
	Renel	adult m		

Comic Scenes for Two Female Characters

Title	Character	Type	Language	Page
All Is True	Anne Boleyn	young w	verse	90
	Old Lady	adult char w		
All's Well That Ends Well	Helen	young w	verse	32
	Countess	adult char w		
All's Well That Ends Well	Helen	young w	verse	32
	Widow	adult char w		
Henry V	Princess	young w	French prose	82
	Alice	adult char w		
The Merchant of Venice	Portia	young w	prose	28
	Nerissa	young char w		
The Merry Wives of Windsor	Mrs. Page	adult w	prose	17
	Mrs. Ford	adult w		
Romeo and Juliet	Juliet	young w	verse	49
	Nurse	adult char w		
Twelfth Night	Viola} (2)	young w	verse	16
	Olivia}	adult char w		
Two Gentlemen of Verona	Julia	young w	verse	2
	Lucetta	young char w		
Two Gentlemen of Verona	Julia	young w	verse	2
	Sylvia	young w		
Catiline	Fulvia	adult w	verse	67
	Galla	young char w		
Gallathea	Phillida	young w	prose	11
	Gallathea	young w		

Comic Scenes by Shakespeare for One Female and One Male Character

Title	Character	Type	Language	Page
All's Well That Ends Well	Helen	young w	prose	32
	Parolles	adult char m		
All's Well That Ends Well	Helen	young w	verse	32
	Bertram	young m		
Antony and Cleopatra	Cleopatra	adult w	verse	61
	Messenger	young char m		
As You Like It	Rosalind} (2)	young w	prose	15
	Orlando}	young m		
The Comedy of Errors	Luciana	young w	verse	4
	Antipholus S.	adult m		
Cymbeline	Cloten	young char m	mixed	99
	Innogen	young w		
1 Henry IV	Hotspur	young char m	verse	79
	Lady Percy	young w		
Henry V	Henry V	adult m	prose	82
	Princess	young w	(incl French)	
1 Henry VI	Suffolk	adult char m	verse	83
	Margaret	adult w		
3 Henry VI	Edward	adult m	verse	86
	Lady Anne	young w		
The Merchant of Venice	Portia	young w	verse	28
	Bassanio	young m		
The Merchant of Venice	Jessica	young w	verse	28
	Lorenzo	young m		
A Midsummer Night's Dream	Helena	young char w	verse	7
	Demetrius	young char m		
A Midsummer Night's Dream	Puck	young char m?	verse	7
	Fairy	young char w?		
Much Ado About Nothing	Beatrice} (3)	adult char w	prose	13
	Benedick}	adult char m		
Romeo and Juliet	Romeo	young m	prose	49
	Nurse	adult char w		
The Taming of the Shrew	Kate	adult char w	verse	5
	Petruccio	adult char m		
The Taming of the Shrew	Kate	adult char w	verse	5
	Petruccio	adult char m		

Title	Character	Type	Language	Page
The Tempest	Miranda} (2)	young w	verse	103
	Ferdinand} (3)	young m		
Troilus and Cressida	Cressida	young w	prose	29
	Pandarus	adult char m		
Twelfth Night	Viola} (2)	young w	verse	16
	Duke}	adult m		
Twelfth Night	Viola	young w	prose	16
	Feste	adult char m		
The Winter's Tale	Perdita	young w	verse	101
	Florizel	young m		

Comic Scenes by Other Dramatists for One Female and One Male Character

Title	Character	Type	Language	Page
1 *The Fair Maid of the West*	Bess Roughman	young w adult char m	verse	27
1 *The Fair Maid of the West*	Bess Goodlack	young w adult m	verse	27
2 *The Fair Maid of the West*	Tota Roughman	adult char w adult char m	verse	27
2 *The Fair Maid of the West*	Spencer Bess	young m young w	verse	27
1 *The Honest Whore*	Viola Fustigo	adult char w adult char m	verse	23
2 *The Honest Whore*	Infelice Orlando	young w adult char m	verse	23
2 *The Honest Whore*	Infelice Hippolito	young w adult m	verse	23
James IV	Dorothea Nano	young w adult char m	verse	12
Philaster	Philaster Bellario/ Euphrasia	young m young w	verse	108
The Witch of Edmonton	Mother Sawyer Devil	adult char w adult char m	prose	109
The Witch of Edmonton	Mother Sawyer Cuddy Banks	adult char w young char m	prose	109

Comic Scenes by Shakespeare for Two Male Characters

Title	Character	Type	Language	Page
As You Like It	Corin	adult char m	prose	15
	Touchstone	adult char m		
As You Like It	Adam	adult char m	verse	15
	Orlando	young m		
The Comedy of Errors	Antipholus S.	adult m	verse	4
	Dromio E.	young char m		
The Comedy of Errors	Antipholus S.}(2)	adult m	prose	4
	Dromio S.}	young char m		
Cymbeline	Giacomo	adult char m	prose	99
	Posthumus	young m		
Hamlet	1 Gravedigger	adult char m	prose	50
	2 Gravedigger	adult char m		
Hamlet	1 Gravedigger	adult char m	prose	50
	Hamlet	adult m		
1 Henry IV	Prince Hal	young m	prose	79
	Falstaff	adult char m		
1 Henry IV	Prince Hal	young m	prose	79
	Falstaff	adult char m		
2 Henry IV	Falstaff	adult char m	prose	80
	Lord Chief Justice	adult m		
2 Henry IV	Prince Hal	young m	prose	80
	Poins	young char m		
2 Henry IV	Silence	adult char m	prose	80
	Shallow	adult char m		
Love's Labour's Lost	Biron	young char m	prose	6
	Costard	adult char m		
Love's Labour's Lost	Don Armado} (2)	adult char m	prose	6
	Mote}	boy		
Measure for Measure	Lucio	adult char m	prose	31
	Duke	adult char m		
The Merchant of Venice	Antonio	adult m	verse	28
	Bassanio	young m		
The Merchant of Venice	Launcelot	young char m	prose	28
	Old Gobbo	adult char m		
The Merry Wives of Windsor	Falstaff} (2)	adult char m	prose	17
	Ford}	adult m		

Title	Character	Type	Language	Page
A Midsummer Night's Dream	Oberon	adult m	verse	7
	Puck	young char		
Romeo and Juliet	Romeo	young m	verse	49
	Mercutio	young m		
The Taming of the Shrew	Lucentio	young m	verse	5
	Tranio	young char m		
The Tempest	Prospero	adult m	verse	103
	Ariel	young char		
Troilus and Cressida	Troilus	young m	mixed	29
	Pandarus	adult char m		
Troilus and Cressida	Ulysses	adult m	verse	29
	Achilles	adult m		
Twelfth Night	Feste	adult char m	prose	16
	Malvolio	adult char m		
Two Gentlemen of Verona	Valentine	young m	verse	2
	Proteus	young m		
Two Gentlemen of Verona	Proteus	young m	prose	2
	Speed	adult char m		
Two Gentlemen of Verona	Speed	adult char m	prose	2
	Valentine	young m		
Two Gentlemen of Verona	Speed} (2)	adult char m	prose	2
	Lance}	adult char m		
The Winter's Tale	Shepherd	adult char m	prose	101
	Clown	young char m		
The Winter's Tale	Autolycus	adult char m	prose	101
	Clown	young char m		

Comic Scenes by Other Dramatists for Two Male Characters

Title	Character	Type	Language	Page
Endimion	Sir Tophas	adult char m	prose	10
	Epiton	boy		
Epicoene	Truewit	adult m	prose	22
	La Foole	adult char m		
2 The Fair Maid of the West	Roughman	adult char m	verse	27
	Goodlack	adult m		
2 The Fair Maid of the West	Mullisheg	adult char m	verse	27
	Goodlack	adult m		
Friar Bacon and Friar Bungay	Miles	young char m	verse	12
	Devil	young char ?		
1 The Honest Whore	Hippolito	young m	verse	23
	Doctor	adult m		
A King and No King	Mardonius	adult m	prose	108
	Bessus	adult char m		
A King and No King	Bacurius	adult m	prose	108
	Bessus	adult char m		
A King and No King	Arbaces	young m	mixed	108
	Bessus	adult char m		
A New Way to Pay Old Debts	Allworth	young m	verse	38
	Wellborn	adult char m		
Volpone	Mosca	young char m	verse	21
	Corvino	adult char m		
The White Devil	Flamineo	adult char m	mixed	70
	Camillo	adult char m		

Comic Scenes for Three Characters

Title	Character	Type	Language	Page
As You Like It	Rosalind	young w	verse	15
	Celia	young w		
	Duke Frederick	adult m		
As You Like It	Rosalind	young w	mixed	15
	Phebe	young char w		
	Silvius	young char m		
Henry V	Gower	adult char m	prose	82
	Fluellen	adult char m		
	Pistol	adult char m		
The Merchant of Venice	Shylock	adult char m	verse	28
	Antonio	adult m		
	Bassanio	young m		
The Merry Wives of Windsor	Falstaff	adult char m	prose	17
	Mrs. Page	adult w		
	Mrs. Ford	adult w		
Much Ado About Nothing	Hero	young w	verse	13
	Ursula	young char w		
	Beatrice	adult char w		
The Tempest	Trinculo	adult char m	prose	103
	Stephano	adult char m		
	Caliban	adult char m		
Troilus and Cressida	Troilus	young m	mixed	29
	Cressida	young w		
	Pandarus	adult char m		
A New Way to Pay Old Debts	Overreach	adult char m	verse	38
	Margaret	young w		
	Justice Greedy	adult char m		
Volpone	Volpone	adult char m	verse	21
	Mosca	young char m		
	Voltore	adult char m		